GREAT TASTES

ITALIAN

First published in 2009 by Bay Books, an imprint of Murdoch Books Pty Limited
This edition published in 2010.

Murdoch Books Australia
Pier 8/9
23 Hickson Road
Millers Point NSW 2000
Phone: +61 (0) 2 8220 2000
Fax: +61 (0) 2 8220 2558
www.murdochbooks.com.au

Murdoch Books UK Limited
Erico House, 6th Floor
93–99 Upper Richmond Road
Putney, London SW15 2TG
Phone: +44 (0) 20 8785 5995
Fax: +44 (0) 20 8785 5985
www.murdochbooks.co.uk

Chief Executive: Juliet Rogers
Publishing Director: Kay Scarlett
Publisher: Lynn Lewis
Senior Designer: Heather Menzies
Designer: Wendy Inkster
Production: Kita George
Index: Jo Rudd

ISBN: 9781741965803

PRINTED IN CHINA

IMPORTANT: Those who might be at risk from the effects of salmonella poisoning (the elderly, pregnant women, young children and those suffering from immune deficiency diseases) should consult their doctor with any concerns about eating raw eggs.

OVEN GUIDE: You may find cooking times vary depending on the oven you are using. For fan-forced ovens, as a general rule, set the oven temperature to 20°C (35°F) lower than indicated in the recipe.

GREAT TASTES

ITALIAN

More than 120 easy recipes for every day

bay books

CONTENTS

ANTIPASTO & SOUPS

BRUSCHETTA

MAKES 12

BRUSCHETTA

6 large slices country-style bread, halved

1 garlic clove

extra virgin olive oil

TOMATO AND BASIL BRUSCHETTA

4 ripe tomatoes

1 tablespoon shredded basil

4 pieces bruschetta

WILD MUSHROOM BRUSCHETTA

2 tablespoons extra virgin olive oil

400 g (14 oz) selection of wild
    mushrooms (such as fresh porcini or
    chestnut mushrooms)

2 garlic cloves, crushed

1 tablespoon chopped thyme

4 pieces bruschetta

EGGPLANT BRUSCHETTA

2 eggplants (aubergines), sliced

2 garlic cloves, crushed

150 ml (5 fl oz) extra virgin olive oil

juice of 1 small lemon

3 tablespoons roughly chopped mint

4 pieces bruschetta

1 To make the basic bruschetta, grill (broil), chargrill or toast the bread until it is light brown. Peel the garlic clove and rub over both sides of the bread, then drizzle a little extra virgin olive oil over each slice.

2 To make the tomato and basil bruschetta, roughly chop the tomatoes and mix with the basil. Season well and pile onto the bruschetta.

3 To make the wild mushroom bruschetta, heat the olive oil in a large saucepan or frying pan. When the oil is hot, add just enough mushrooms to cover the base of the pan and cook them over high heat, stirring frequently. Season with salt and pepper. (Sometimes the mushrooms can become watery when cooked. Continue cooking until all the liquid has evaporated.) Add a little crushed garlic and thyme and cook for another minute. Remove from the pan and repeat with the remaining mushrooms. Spoon over the bruschetta and serve warm.

4 To make the eggplant topping, heat a chargrill pan on the stovetop and cook the eggplant slices, a few at a time, over high heat until soft and cooked, turning once. Mix together the garlic, oil, lemon juice and mint and season well. Put the eggplant in a dish with the marinade and leave for 30 minutes. Place a couple of pieces of eggplant on each bruschetta and spoon the marinade over the top.

DEEP-FRIED ZUCCHINI FLOWERS

SERVES 4

12 zucchini (courgette) flowers

BATTER

50 g (1¾ oz) plain (all-purpose) flour

2 teaspoons olive oil

3 egg whites

oil, for deep-frying

lemon wedges, to serve

1 **Check the zucchini flowers are clean** and aren't hiding any insects. Trim the stems to about 2 cm (¾ inch).

2 **To make the batter,** sift the flour into a bowl and stir in ¼ teaspoon salt. Mix in the oil with a wooden spoon, then slowly add 75–100 ml (2¼–3½ fl oz) warm water to make a smooth thick batter. Whisk the egg whites until stiff peaks form, then fold gently into the batter.

3 **Fill a deep-fryer** or deep pan one-third full with oil and heat to about 180°C (350°F), or until a piece of bread fries golden brown in 15 seconds. If the oil starts to smoke, it is too hot.

4 **Dip the zucchini flowers** into the batter, coating them completely. Fry in batches until golden brown, turning once to cook on both sides. Drain on paper towels, sprinkle with salt and serve immediately with lemon wedges.

BAGNA CAODA

SERVES 4

40 pieces assorted raw vegetables, such as carrot, celery, fennel, capsicum (pepper) and cauliflower florets

200 ml (7 fl oz) olive oil

6 garlic cloves, crushed

120 g (4¼ oz) anchovy fillets, finely chopped

90 g (3¼ oz) butter

country-style bread, such as ciabatta

1 Trim, wash and dry the vegetables and cut them into suitably sized pieces for dipping.

2 Put the oil, garlic and anchovies in a saucepan and place over medium heat. Cook gently, stirring once or twice, until the anchovies dissolve. Be careful that the garlic does not brown or it will taste bitter. Add the butter and leave over low heat, stirring once or twice until it has melted. Season with pepper.

3 Transfer the sauce to a bowl and keep it warm at the table by placing on a food warmer or over a burner or spirit stove (a fondue dish works well for this). Serve the vegetables and bread arranged on a platter.

4 To eat, dip your choice of vegetable into the hot bagna caôda and use a piece of bread to catch drips.

CARPACCIO

SERVES 6

700 g (1 lb 9 oz) good-quality beef fillet
1 egg yolk
3 teaspoons Dijon mustard
3 tablespoons lemon juice
2 drops Tabasco
75 ml (2¼ fl oz) olive oil
1 tablespoon cream
2–3 tablespoons capers, rinsed

1 **The easiest way to slice** your beef very thinly is to firm it up in the freezer first. Wrap the piece of beef tightly in plastic wrap, keeping it in a nice block, and put it in the freezer for about 30 minutes or until it feels firm when you prod it.

2 **Using a very sharp knife** with a long blade or a mandolin, cut the beef into paper-thin slices. These slices should be so thin that you can almost see through them. Don't worry about the odd hole or tear.

3 **As you slice,** lay the meat out on six serving plates, arranging the pieces in a thin even layer. Cover with plastic wrap until you are ready to serve, making sure the plastic wrap is pressed to the surface of the meat so it can't oxidise and turn brown.

4 **Blend the egg yolk,** mustard, lemon juice and Tabasco with a whisk, blender or food processor. Add the olive oil in a very thin stream, whisking or processing continuously until the mayonnaise thickens. When you have added all the oil, whisk in the cream. Season to taste with salt and white pepper.

5 **Drizzle the dressing** over the beef just before you serve and sprinkle each plate with capers.

CROSTINI

MAKES 50

CROSTINI

2 day-old country-style bread

200 ml (7 fl oz) extra virgin olive oil

TAPENADE CROSTINI

250 g (9 oz) whole black olives, pitted

50 g (1¾ oz) anchovy fillets

1 tablespoon capers, drained

2 garlic cloves, crushed

1 small handful basil, finely chopped

grated zest and juice of 1 lemon

200 ml (7 fl oz) extra virgin olive oil

RED CAPSICUM CROSTINI

3 tablespoons extra virgin olive oil

1 onion, finely chopped

2 red capsicum (peppers), thinly sliced

2 garlic cloves, crushed

1 tablespoon capers, drained and chopped

2 tablespoons balsamic vinegar

1 tablespoon chopped parsley

CHICKEN LIVER CROSTINI

200 g (7 oz) chicken livers

3 tablespoons olive oil

1 small onion, finely chopped

2 garlic cloves, crushed

1 tablespoon finely chopped sage

2 tablespoons dry Marsala

2 tablespoons mascarpone

1   To make the crostini, preheat the oven to 180°C (350°F/ Gas 4). Thinly slice the bread, cut each piece into quarters and drizzle olive oil over both sides. Lightly toast the bread in the oven until just crisp. The crostini will keep in an airtight container for at least a couple of days once completely cooled.

2   To make the tapenade crostini, finely chop the olives, anchovies and capers together with a knife or food processor and put them in a bowl. Add the garlic, basil, lemon zest and juice, stir in the olive oil and season well. Spread on the crostini to serve. (The tapenade will keep in an airtight container in the fridge for up to a month if sealed with a layer of olive oil.)

3   To make the red capsicum crostini, heat the olive oil in a frying pan and cook the onion for a few minutes until soft. Add the capsicum and cook for a further 15 minutes, stirring frequently. Season, then add the garlic and cook for another minute. Add the capers and vinegar and simmer gently for a few minutes to reduce the liquid. Add the parsley just before spreading onto the crostini.

4   To make the chicken liver crostini, trim the chicken livers of any sinew. Heat the olive oil in a frying pan and gently cook the onion for 2 minutes until soft. Push the onion to the side, increase the heat and add the livers. Cook until they are lightly brown on both sides, then add the garlic and sage and cook for 1 minute. Add the Marsala and cook briefly to reduce the liquid. Season well. Chop to a paste in a food processor or by hand, then add the mascarpone. The chicken liver can be served warm or chilled on the crostini.

MEAT ANTIPASTO

SERVES 6

700 g (1 lb 9 oz) good-quality beef fillet

1 egg yolk

3 teaspoons Dijon mustard

3 tablespoons lemon juice

2 drops Tabasco

75 ml (2¼ fl oz) olive oil

1 tablespoon cream

2–3 tablespoons capers, rinsed

6 slices lardo (cured pork fat)

6 slices felino salami or 1 or 2 cacciatore salami

6 slices coppa di parma

6 slices bresaola

6 slices prosciutto di Parma or San Daniele

6 plain olive oil bruschetta (see page 8)

6 slices mortadella

6 chicken liver crostini (see page 12)

black olives, in brine and unpitted

pickled baby onions (cipollini)

caperberries

sun-dried tomatoes

3 figs, halved

6 slices cantaloupe melon

country-style bread, such as ciabatta, to serve

extra virgin olive oil and lemon juice, to serve

Called affettati misti in Italian, the platter should be made up of a good selection of meats that contrast in flavour and appearance. Serve with fruit such as figs, olives and caperberries, or with slices of ripe melon or pear.

A meat antipasto plate is probably the quickest to put together. It is, however, very important that you choose a really good selection of meats. Buy the best quality you can afford: the fresher the meat is, the better it will taste. If you are planning on serving this dish often, you may want to buy a few whole salami and slice them yourself as you need them.

Meat is best served with strong accompaniments such as caperberries, cipollini and olives, which cut through any fattiness, or with sweet fruit like figs and melon that enhance its flavours.

To put together an attractive platter, cut the meat in different ways. The lardo needs to be sliced very thinly, almost shaved. The salami can be sliced according to your personal taste—generally the smaller salami such as cacciatore are cut into thicker slices than the large ones. Mortadella is often cut into cubes instead of slicing.

Lay out the meats on a platter, folding some and rolling others. Arrange a choice of the accompaniments on the platter with them so your guests can help themselves, and serve with plenty of bread. The bresaola should be sprinkled with a little olive oil and lemon juice just before you serve. Always serve a meat antipasto platter at room temperature—meat taken straight from the fridge will not have as much flavour.

VEGETABLE ANTIPASTO

SERVES 6

150 g (5½ oz) cooked asparagus spears, refreshed in cold water

grilled vegetable salad or ready-made grilled capsicum (pepper), eggplant (aubergine) and zucchini (courgette)

18 ready-made sun-dried tomatoes

6 stuffed artichokes or 6 ready-made marinated artichoke hearts

12 ready-made marinated mushrooms

12 ready-made marinated onions

6 arrancini (see page 58)

6 tapenade or red capsicum (pepper) crostini (see page 12)

a selection of marinated olives

lemon wedges, to serve

extra virgin olive oil, to serve

grissini (see page 127) or country-style bread, such as ciabatta, to serve

Vegetable antipasto plates can be as much or as little work as you like. You can either put together a collection of the suggested recipes from this book or you can buy ready-prepared ingredients from delicatessens or supermarkets. Alternatively, make some of the recipes and supplement these with some bought items.

Choose from the suggested list, basing your selection on flavour, colour and compatibility. If you like crostini, then choose both types, or add a version of your own. If you don't have much time, pick easy things to make such as the asparagus or, quicker still, buy them. You can buy perfectly acceptable antipasto vegetables such as grilled capsicum, eggplant, courgettes and sun-dried tomatoes at delicatessens, as well as marinated artichoke hearts, mushrooms, onions and olives.

To make an attractive antipasto course, choose either one large platter or several small plates or bowls—it is better to spread things out rather than trying to cram them all in together. The crostini and grissini can be served on one plate, but if something is served in a sauce or if the individual vegetables have different herbs and flavourings they will probably be best served in individual bowls to prevent a confusion of flavours. Serve plenty of bread and grissini to accompany the antipasto (especially if you are serving it as a meal in itself) as well as extra olive oil and lemon wedges for dressing.

SEAFOOD ANTIPASTO

SERVES 6

6 sardines or similar fish, gutted,
   scaled and grilled, or sardine fillets

6 salt cod fritters (see page 69)

1 quantity garlic prawns (see page 67) or
   bought cooked prawns

1 quantity octopus salad (see page 66)
   or ready-prepared marinated octopus

grilled mixed shellfish

1 quantity sole in saor (see page 70)

marinated anchovies (see page 64)
   or tinned anchovies

ready-prepared marinated mussels

FRITTO MISTO DI MARE

50 g (1¾ oz) plain (all-purpose) flour

2 teaspoons olive oil

3 egg whites

600 g (1 lb 5 oz) mixed cleaned prawns,
   squid rings and scallops

oil, for deep-frying

lemon wedges, to serve

finely chopped parsley, to serve

country-style bread, such as ciabatta,
   to serve

Choose a selection of seafood from the list—you can serve as many or as few as you want, but four is probably a manageable number. If you are going to use fresh fish and grill them, make sure that they really are fresh. Heat the grill to its highest setting and brush each fish with olive oil. Grill the fish on both sides until they are cooked through.

Marinated fish can be bought in jars and tins or from delicatessens. Choose anchovies and sardines in salt or olive oil rather than vegetable oil. Rinse and pat them dry, then arrange in a dish and sprinkle them with lemon juice and chopped parsley (add a little chopped garlic if you like). Cooked prawns are best bought in their shells and peeled at home, or buy raw ones and cook them yourself if you prefer.

If you have time, make a selection of the suggested recipes for your platter. If not, you can buy everything you need ready-prepared. Bear in mind that when you serve fish and shellfish you will need plenty of lemon to cut through any oil and lots of bread for mopping up juices.

To make the fritto misto di mare, first make the batter. Sift the flour into a bowl and stir in ¼ teaspoon salt. Mix in the oil, then slowly add 75–100 ml (2¼–3½ fl oz) warm water to make a smooth thick batter. Whisk the egg whites until stiff peaks form, then fold gently into the batter.

Fill a deep-fryer or large saucepan one-third full with oil and heat to 180°C (350°F), or until a piece of bread fries golden brown in 20 seconds. If the oil starts to smoke, it is too hot.

Dip the seafood into the batter, coating all sides. Fry in batches until the batter is crisp. Remove with a slotted spoon or tongs and drain on paper towel. Season with salt and serve immediately with lemon wedges.

BOTTARGA

SERVES 4

BOTTARGA WITH OLIVE OIL

200 g (7 oz) bottarga (salted, dried fish roe)

2 tablespoons extra virgin olive oil

4 lemon wedges

4 slices country-style bread

extra virgin olive oil and lemon wedges, to serve

BOTTARGA WITH SCRAMBLED EGGS

50 g (1¾ oz) bottarga

8 eggs

1 tablespoon olive oil

4 slices country-style bread

1 Slice the bottarga with a sharp knife or mandolin. Cut it into enough slices to arrange a thin layer on four dinner plates.

2 To serve the bottarga with olive oil, drizzle half a teaspoon of oil and squeeze a lemon wedge over each plate. Serve immediately (or the lemon will discolour the bottarga) with bread, olive oil and lemon.

3 To serve the bottarga with scrambled eggs, lightly beat the eggs together, and season with pepper only (the bottarga is very salty). Preheat the serving bowls by filling them with boiling water. Leave to stand for a few minutes before drying. Slice half the bottarga, as above, and store the rest in the fridge, tightly wrapped.

4 Heat the oil in a saucepan and add the eggs. Turn the heat down to low and gently scramble the eggs until they are creamy but not completely set. Tip the eggs into the serving bowls and put the bottarga on top where it will soften. Serve with the bread.

MINESTRONE ALLA GENOVESE

SERVES 6

220 g (7¾ oz) dried borlotti beans

50 g (1¾ oz) lard or extra virgin olive oil

1 large onion, finely chopped

1 garlic clove, finely chopped

2 celery stalks, halved then sliced

2 carrots, sliced

1 small handful flat-leaf (Italian) parsley, finely chopped

2 sage leaves

100 g (3½ oz) pancetta, cubed

3 potatoes, peeled but left whole

400 g (14 oz) tinned chopped tomatoes

8 basil leaves

3 litres (102 fl oz/12 cups) chicken stock

PESTO

2 garlic cloves

50 g (1¾ oz) pine nuts

120 g (4¼ oz) basil, stems removed

180 ml (6 fl oz/¾ cup) olive oil

50 g (1¾ oz) parmesan cheese, grated

2 zucchini (courgettes), sliced

220 g (7¾ oz) peas

120 g (4¼ oz) runner beans, trimmed

¼ cabbage, shredded

150 g (5½ oz) ditalini

grated parmesan cheese, to serve

1 Put the dried beans in a large bowl, cover with cold water and leave to soak overnight. Drain and rinse well.

2 To make the soffritto (base flavouring) melt the lard in a large saucepan and add the onion, garlic, celery, carrot, parsley, sage and pancetta. Cook over low heat, stirring occasionally, for about 10 minutes, or until the onion is soft and golden.

3 Add the potatoes and cook very gently for 15 minutes. Stir in the tomatoes, basil and borlotti beans. Season with plenty of pepper. Add the stock and bring to the boil. Cover and leave to simmer for 2 hours, stirring occasionally.

4 To make the pesto, put the garlic and pine nuts in a mortar and pestle or food processor and pound or process until finely chopped. Add the basil and olive oil and pound or process until the basil is puréed. Season and mix in the parmesan by hand. Put the pesto in a jar and cover the surface with a layer of olive oil to stop it discolouring.

5 If the potatoes haven't already broken up, use a fork to roughly crush them against the side of the pan. Taste for seasoning and add the courgettes, peas, runner beans, cabbage and pasta. Simmer until the pasta is al dente.

6 Serve with a spoonful of pesto and plenty of parmesan.

LA RIBOLITA

SERVES 4

4 tablespoons olive oil

1 onion, finely chopped

1 large carrot

3 celery stalks

2 garlic cloves, crushed

250 g (9 oz) cavolo nero or savoy
  cabbage

1 zucchini (courgette), finely chopped

400 g (14 oz) cooked cannellini or
  borlotti beans

400 g (14 oz) tinned peeled tomatoes

1 whole dried chilli

200 ml (7 fl oz) red wine

1 litre (35 fl oz/4 cups) chicken stock

75 g (2½ oz) stale country-style bread,
  such as ciabatta or pugliese, crusts
  removed and broken into 2.5 cm
  (1 inch) pieces

extra virgin olive oil, to serve

1 **To make the soffritto** (base flavouring), pour the oil into a large saucepan and first add the onion. Cook the onion gently over low heat. While the onion is cooking, finely chop the carrot and celery and add them to the saucepan as you go along. Add the garlic, then leave to cook for a few minutes.

2 **Strip the leaves** of the cavolo nero from the stems or cut away the thick stem of the savoy cabbage. Wash and finely chop the stems and roughly chop the leaves. Add the cabbage stems and zucchini to the soffritto and cook, stirring occasionally, for about 5 minutes, or until the vegetables are translucent and have soaked up some of the olive oil.

3 **Stir in the beans** and cook for 5 minutes more, then add the tomatoes and chilli and cook for 5 minutes to reduce the liquid.

4 **Add the cabbage leaves** and mix into the soup, stirring until just wilted. Add the wine and stock and gently simmer for about 40 minutes.

5 **Add the bread** to the pan (if the bread is fresh, cut it into the pieces and then dry it out a little in the oven first to stop it disintegrating into the soup). Mix briefly and remove the pan from the heat. Leave for about 30 minutes to rest. Serve hot but not boiling with a generous drizzle of extra virgin olive oil (you may want to remove the chilli before you serve the soup).

PAPPA AL POMODORO

900 g (2 lb) very ripe tomatoes or 800 g (1 lb 12 oz) tinned chopped tomatoes

3 tablespoons olive oil

3 garlic cloves, finely sliced

200 g (7 oz) stale country-style bread, such as ciabatta, crusts removed

1 small handful basil, torn into large pieces

50 ml (1¾ fl oz) extra virgin olive oil, plus extra to serve

1 **If using fresh tomatoes**, remove the stems and score a cross in the bottom of each one. Blanch in boiling water for 30 seconds. Transfer to cold water, peel the skin away from the cross (it should slip off easily) and chop the tomatoes.

2 **Pour the olive oil** into a large heavy-based saucepan, add the garlic and cook gently until light golden brown. Add the tomatoes, taking care as the oil may spit. Season with salt and pepper.

3 **Bring the tomatoes to the boil** and gently simmer, stirring occasionally so they don't stick. Simmer for about 10 minutes, stirring more frequently, until the mixture has thickened.

4 **Break the bread into chunks** and add to the pan. Remove from the heat and stir briefly to coat the bread with the tomato mixture. Scatter with the basil, season with salt and pepper and pour 500 ml (17 fl oz/2 cups) boiling water over the bread. Add the olive oil and stir a little, being careful not to break up the bread too much.

5 **Leave to rest** for 5 minutes before serving. Serve in hot bowls with an extra drizzle of oil on top.

CHESTNUT, PANCETTA AND CABBAGE SOUP

SERVES 4

200 g (7 oz) cavolo nero or savoy cabbage

2 tablespoons olive oil

1 onion, finely chopped

130 g (4½ oz) pancetta or smoked bacon, diced

2 garlic cloves, chopped

2 tablespoons rosemary, finely chopped

200 g (7 oz) cooked, peeled chestnuts, roughly chopped

200 ml (7 fl oz) red wine

4 crostini (see page 12)

extra virgin olive oil and grated parmesan cheese, to serve

1 Remove any thick stems from the cavolo nero and roughly chop the leaves. Wash well and cook in 1.5 litres (52 fl oz/6 cups) of boiling water for about 10 minutes, or until the stems are tender. Drain in a colander over a large bowl to reserve the cooking water.

2 Using the same saucepan, heat the olive oil and cook the onion and pancetta over medium-high heat until the onion is soft and the pancetta lightly browned. Add the garlic and rosemary and cook for a few more minutes.

3 Add the chestnuts and stir to infuse the flavours, then add the cabbage and season with salt and pepper. Add the wine, bring to the boil and cook for a couple of minutes. Finally add the reserved cabbage water, bring to the boil and then simmer for 10 minutes.

4 Purée one-third of the soup, leaving the remainder unpuréed to give the dish a little texture. Serve the soup hot with crostini on top, drizzled with a little olive oil and sprinkled with parmesan.

BEAN AND BARLEY SOUP

SERVES 4

200 g (7 oz) dried borlotti beans	
2 tablespoons olive oil	
1 small onion, thinly sliced	
2 garlic cloves, crushed	
1.5 litres (52 fl oz/6 cups) chicken stock	
1 tablespoon finely chopped thyme or sage	
200 g (7 oz) pearl barley	
100 g (3½ oz) parmesan cheese, grated	
1 tablespoon finely chopped parsley	
4 teaspoons extra virgin olive oil	

1 Soak the borlotti beans in cold water overnight. Drain off the water and put the beans in a large saucepan with plenty of cold water. Bring to the boil and simmer until tender (this will take about 1½ hours depending on the age of the beans—older drier beans may take longer to soften). Drain.

2 Heat the olive oil in a large saucepan and cook the onion over low heat for 6 minutes, or until soft. Season with salt and pepper. Add the garlic and cook without browning for 20–30 seconds. Add the stock and thyme or sage and bring to the boil.

3 Stir in the barley a little at a time so that the stock continues to boil, then lower the heat and simmer for 15 minutes. Add the borlotti beans and simmer for 30 minutes, or until the barley is tender and the soup is thick.

4 Purée one-third of the soup until smooth, leaving the remainder unpuréed to give the soup a little texture. Return to the saucepan and stir in the parmesan and parsley. Season and stir in 125–250 ml (4–9 fl oz/½–1 cup) hot water to give a spoonable consistency. Serve immediately, with a teaspoon of extra virgin olive oil stirred through each bowl.

PASTA & GNOCCHI

SPAGHETTINI WITH GARLIC AND OIL

SERVES 4

500 g (1 lb 2 oz) spaghettini

90 ml (3 fl oz) extra virgin olive oil

5 garlic cloves, crushed

pinch of dried chilli flakes

2 tablespoons finely chopped flat-leaf
   (Italian) parsley

grated pecorino cheese, to serve

1   Cook the pasta in a large saucepan of boiling salted water until al dente.

2   Meanwhile, heat the oil in a large frying pan over very low heat. Add the garlic and chilli flakes and fry gently for about 2 minutes, or until the garlic has softened but not browned. Remove from the heat.

3   Drain the pasta briefly, leaving some of the water clinging to the pasta. Add the hot pasta and parsley to the frying pan and toss to coat. Taste for seasoning and serve at once with the grated pecorino.

CLASSIC TOMATO SAUCE WITH PENNE

SERVES 4

2 tablespoons extra virgin olive oil
2 garlic cloves, thinly sliced
1 tablespoon chopped herbs, such as thyme, rosemary or basil
800 g (1 lb 12 oz) tomatoes
500 g (1 lb 2 oz) penne
grated parmesan cheese, to serve

1   Heat the olive oil and add the garlic and thyme or rosemary. If using basil, add at the end. Cook until the garlic just browns, then add the tomatoes. Season and break up the tomatoes with the edge of a spoon.

2   Simmer for 20–30 minutes or until the sauce thickens. Stir occasionally to stop it sticking to the pan.

3   Cook the pasta in a large pan of boiling salted water until al dente. Drain. Stir the basil into the sauce, taste for seasoning and serve over the pasta with the grated parmesan.

Note: In Italy this sauce is generally made with tinned tomatoes, but ripe fresh peeled tomatoes can be used if they have a good flavour. Toss the sauce through pasta (either spaghetti or a ridged tube pasta such as penne or rigatoni), use in lasagnes and baked dishes or serve with polenta.

TRENETTE WITH GENOVESE PESTO SAUCE

SERVES 4

PESTO

2 garlic cloves

50 g (1¾ oz) pine nuts

120 g (4¼ oz) basil, stems removed

150-180 ml (5–6 fl oz) extra virgin olive oil

50 g (1¾ oz) parmesan cheese, finely grated, plus extra to serve

500 g (1 lb 2 oz) trenette

175 g (6 oz) green beans, trimmed

175 g (6 oz) small potatoes, very thinly sliced

1 **Put the garlic** and pine nuts in a mortar and pestle or food processor and pound or process until finely ground. Add the basil, then drizzle in the olive oil a little at a time while pounding or processing. When you have a thick purée stop adding the oil. Season and mix in the parmesan.

2 **Bring a large saucepan** of salted water to the boil. Add the pasta, green beans and potatoes, stirring well to prevent the pasta from sticking together. Cook until the pasta is al dente (the vegetables should be cooked by this time), then drain, reserving a little of the water.

3 **Return the pasta** and vegetables to the saucepan, add the pesto, and mix well. If necessary, add some of the reserved water to loosen the pasta. Season and serve immediately with the extra parmesan.

TAGLIATELLE WITH RAGÙ

SERVES 4

60 g (2¼ oz) butter

90 g (3¼ oz) pancetta, finely chopped

1 onion, finely chopped

1 celery stalk, finely chopped

1 carrot, finely chopped

220 g (7¾ oz) minced (ground) beef

220 g (7¾ oz) minced (ground) pork

2 oregano sprigs, chopped, or
   ¼ teaspoon dried oregano

pinch of ground nutmeg

120 g (4¼ oz) chicken livers, trimmed
   and finely chopped

125 ml (4 fl oz/½ cup) milk

125 ml (4 fl oz/½ cup) dry white wine

400 g (14 oz) tinned chopped tomatoes

250 ml (9 fl oz/1 cup) beef stock

350 g (12 oz) fresh tagliatelle

3 tablespoons cream

grated parmesan cheese, to serve

1   Heat the butter in a saucepan and add the pancetta. Cook until lightly browned and then add the onion, celery and carrot. Cook over medium heat for 6–8 minutes, stirring from time to time.

2   Add the beef, pork and oregano to the saucepan. Season with the nutmeg and salt and pepper.

3   Cook for about 5 minutes, or until the beef and pork has changed colour but not yet browned. Add the liver and cook until it changes colour.

4   Stir in the milk and simmer for 2 minutes. Pour in the wine, increase the heat and boil over high heat for 2–3 minutes, or until the wine has been absorbed, then reduce the heat and simmer for 10 minutes.

5   Add the tomatoes and half the stock, partially cover the pan and leave to simmer gently over very low heat for 3 hours. Add more of the stock as it is needed to keep the sauce moist.

6   Cook the tagliatelle in a large saucepan of boiling salted water until al dente. Stir the cream into the sauce 5 minutes before serving. Check for seasoning, then drain the tagliatelle briefly, toss with the sauce and serve with grated parmesan.

SPAGHETTI CARBONARA

SERVES 4

1 tablespoon olive oil

250 g (9 oz) pancetta, smoked pancetta or guanciale, cut into small dice

4 tablespoons thick (double/heavy) cream

6 egg yolks

500 g (1 lb 2 oz) spaghetti

50 g (1¾ oz) parmesan cheese, grated, plus extra to serve

1 Put the olive oil in a saucepan and cook the pancetta over medium heat, stirring frequently, until it is light brown and crisp. Tip the pancetta into a metal colander to strain off the fat. Mix together the cream and egg yolks and, when the pancetta has cooled, add it to the egg mixture.

2 Cook the pasta in a large saucepan of boiling salted water until al dente. Drain, reserving a little of the cooking water.

3 Return the pasta to the saucepan to retain as much heat as possible, add the egg mixture and parmesan, season and mix together. Add a little of the reserved water if the sauce is too thick and the pasta is stuck together. The spaghetti should look as if it has a fine coating of egg and cream. Serve immediately with a little extra parmesan sprinkled over the top.

BUCATINI ALL'AMATRICIANA

SERVES 4

100 ml (3½ fl oz) extra virgin olive oil
1 red onion, finely chopped
75 g (2½ oz) pancetta, smoked pancetta or guanciale
1 tablespoon chopped rosemary leaves
2 garlic cloves, chopped
1 large dried chilli (optional)
200 ml (7 fl oz) red wine
800 g (1 lb 12 oz) tinned chopped tomatoes
500 g (1 lb 2 oz) bucatini
grated parmesan cheese, to serve

1 **Heat the olive oil** in a saucepan and cook the onion and pancetta over low heat until they are soft and caramelised, being careful they don't burn. Add the rosemary, garlic and chilli and cook the garlic until light brown.

2 **Add the red wine** and bring to the boil, scraping the bottom of the saucepan for anything that may be stuck to it, as this will give flavour to the sauce. When the wine has reduced, add the tomatoes and simmer gently for about 10 minutes, or until the sauce has reduced and thickened. Remove the chilli.

3 **Cook the pasta** in a large saucepan of boiling salted water until it is al dente. Drain briefly, allowing some of the water to remain clinging to the pasta, then mix with the sauce. Serve with the parmesan sprinkled over the top.

SPAGHETTI ALLA PUTTANESCA

SERVES 4

1 small red chilli

1 tablespoon capers

4 tablespoons olive oil

1 small onion, finely chopped

2 garlic cloves, finely sliced

6 anchovy fillets, finely chopped

400 g (14 oz) tinned chopped tomatoes

1 tablespoon finely chopped oregano
   or ¼ teaspoon dried oregano

100 g (3½ oz) black olives, pitted and
   halved

400 g (14 oz) spaghetti

1 tablespoon finely chopped parsley

1 **Cut the chilli** in half, remove the seeds and then chop it finely. Rinse the capers, squeeze them dry and, if they are large, chop them roughly.

2 **Heat the olive oil** in a large saucepan and add the onion, garlic and chilli. Fry gently for about 6 minutes, or until the onion is soft. Add the anchovies and cook, stirring and mashing, until they break down to a smooth paste.

3 **Add the tomatoes,** oregano, olives and capers and bring to the boil. Reduce the heat, season and leave to simmer for about 10 minutes, or until the sauce has reduced and thickened.

4 **Meanwhile,** cook the pasta in a large saucepan of boiling salted water until al dente. Drain briefly, leaving some of the water still clinging to the pasta, then add to the sauce with the parsley. Toss well before serving.

PASTA ALLA NORMA

SERVES 4

1 large eggplant (aubergine), cut into 2 cm (¾ inch) thick slices
350 g (12 oz) fresh tomatoes or 400 g (14 oz) tinned chopped tomatoes
160 ml (5¼ fl oz) olive oil
2 garlic cloves, thinly sliced
handful of torn basil leaves
400 g (14 oz) conchiglie
150 g (5½ oz) fresh ricotta cheese

1 Put the eggplant slices in a bowl of salted water for 10 minutes.

2 Drain and dry on a tea towel (dish towel).

3 If using fresh tomatoes, remove the stems and score a cross in the bottom of each one. Blanch in boiling water for 30 seconds. Transfer to cold water, peel the skin away from the cross (it should slip off easily) and chop the tomatoes.

4 Put a generous amount of the olive oil in a frying pan and cook the eggplant in batches over medium high heat until golden brown and soft inside, adding more of the oil as you need it. Drain in a colander or on paper towels. Cut the eggplant into 2 cm (¾ inch) thick sticks and set aside.

5 Remove all but 2 tablespoons of the oil from the frying pan, add the garlic and cook until light golden brown. Add the tomatoes and season. Cook until the sauce has reduced and thickened. Add the eggplant and the basil leaves, mix well and set aside.

6 Cook the pasta in a large saucepan of boiling salted water until al dente. Drain briefly, leaving some of the water clinging to the pasta, then return the pasta to the saucepan with the aubergine mixture and 100 g of the ricotta.

7 Mix briefly, check for seasoning and serve immediately with the remaining ricotta crumbled over the top.

PASTA PRIMAVERA

SERVES 4

120 g (4¼ oz) broad beans (500 g/
1 lb 2 oz with pods still on), fresh
or frozen

150 g (5½ oz) asparagus, cut into short
lengths

100 g (3½ oz) green beans, cut into
short lengths

120 g (4¼ oz) peas, fresh or frozen

30 g (1 oz) butter

1 small fennel bulb, thinly sliced

375 ml (13 fl oz) thick (double/heavy)
cream

350 g (12 oz) fresh tagliatelle

2 tablespoons grated parmesan cheese,
plus extra to serve

1 Bring a large saucepan of water to the boil. Add
1 teaspoon salt, the broad beans and asparagus and simmer
for 3 minutes. Remove the vegetables with a slotted spoon
and put them in a sieve. Run under cold water briefly—this
stops them cooking and preserves their bright green colour—
then set aside.

2 Add the green beans and peas to the pan (if using frozen
peas add them a few minutes later). Cook for about 4 minutes,
then remove with a slotted spoon and put in a sieve. Run
under cold water briefly to stop them cooking, then set aside.

3 Peel the tough grey outer skins off the broad beans.

4 Meanwhile, heat the butter in a large frying pan. Add the
fennel and cook over low heat for 5 minutes without letting it
brown at all. Add the cream, season with salt and pepper and
cook at a low simmer for 2 minutes.

5 Bring the large saucepan of water back to the boil, add
the pasta and cook until al dente. Drain the pasta briefly,
leaving some water clinging to the pasta.

6 Add the green beans, peas, parmesan, broad beans
and asparagus to the frying pan and lightly toss together.
Add the pasta and lightly toss to coat with the sauce. Serve
immediately with extra parmesan sprinkled over the top.

RIGATONI WITH SAUSAGE, FENNEL SEED AND TOMATO

SERVES 4

2 garlic cloves, chopped
2 teaspoons fennel seeds
3 tablespoons olive oil
1 onion, finely chopped
4 Italian sausages, skin removed
1 tablespoon chopped thyme leaves
100 ml (3½ fl oz) red wine
400 g (14 oz) tinned chopped tomatoes
400 g (14 oz) rigatoni
grated parmesan cheese, to serve

1 **Using a mortar** and pestle, crush the garlic and fennel seeds with a pinch of salt. Alternatively, grind the seeds in a spice grinder and crush the garlic.

2 **Heat the oil** in a saucepan and cook the onion for a few minutes over low heat to soften it. Break up the sausage meat with your hands and add it to the pan. Increase the heat and cook until the meat is lightly browned. Season with salt and pepper. Add the garlic, fennel and thyme, mix briefly, then add the wine. Stir the sauce, scraping up any sausage meat that may be stuck to the bottom of the pan—this will add flavour to the sauce.

3 **Cook the sauce** for about 5 minutes or until the wine is reduced, then add the tomatoes and simmer for 10 minutes, or until the sauce has thickened.

4 **Cook the pasta** in a large saucepan of boiling salted water until al dente. Drain briefly, leaving some water clinging to the pasta. Add to the sauce, toss well and serve sprinkled with the parmesan.

PASTA AND BEANS

SERVES 4

250 g (9 oz) fresh borlotti beans (450 g/ 1 lb with pods still on) or 400 g (14 oz) tinned

2 tablespoons extra virgin olive oil

1 onion, finely chopped

1 large celery stalk, finely chopped

1 large carrot, finely chopped

100 g (3½ oz) pancetta, diced

2 garlic cloves, finely chopped

1 tablespoon chopped rosemary

½ large red chilli, chopped (optional)

100 ml (3½ fl oz) red wine

4 large peeled tomatoes, chopped or 400 g (14 oz) tinned chopped tomatoes

500 ml (17 fl oz/2 cups) chicken stock or water

150 g (5½ oz) small pasta shapes, such as ditalini, conchiglie or maltagliati

25 g (1 oz) parmesan cheese, grated, plus extra to serve

extra virgin olive oil, to serve

1 Cook the borlotti beans in plenty of boiling water for about 10 minutes, or until they are tender. If using tinned beans, drain and rinse them well.

2 Put the oil in a large saucepan and make the soffritto by cooking the onion, celery and carrot over gentle heat for about 10 minutes. Add the pancetta and increase the heat slightly. Cook for a further 10 minutes, or until the pancetta is lightly browned.

3 Add the garlic, rosemary and chilli, mix well, then reduce the heat and cook for another few minutes. Add the borlotti beans, season and cook for a few minutes, then add the wine and tomatoes. Cook the tomatoes for 15 minutes, or until the sauce has reduced and thickened.

4 Remove about a cup of the mixture and purée it, then return it to the remaining mixture and stir well. The dish can be prepared in advance up to this point and then finished off closer to serving time.

5 Add the chicken stock and bring the sauce to the boil. Add the pasta, season with a little salt and cook until al dente, stirring once or twice to make sure the pieces are not stuck together. Remove from the heat and leave to rest for 5 minutes.

6 Before serving, stir in the parmesan. Serve with extra parmesan scattered over the top and a drizzle of extra virgin olive oil.

SPAGHETTI WITH PRAWNS, CLAMS AND SCALLOPS

SERVES 4

250 ml (8 fl oz/1 cup) dry white wine

pinch of saffron threads

1 kg (2 lb 4 oz) clams (vongole)

4 baby octopus

200 g (7 oz) small squid tubes

500 g (1 lb 2 oz) prawns (shrimp)

6 tomatoes

400 g (14 oz) spaghetti

4 tablespoons olive oil

3 garlic cloves, crushed

8–10 scallops, cleaned

6 tablespoons chopped parsley

lemon wedges, to serve

1 Put the wine and saffron in a bowl and leave to infuse. Clean the clams by scrubbing them thoroughly and scraping off any barnacles. Rinse well under running water and discard any that are broken or open and don't close when tapped on the work surface. Place them in a large saucepan with 185 ml (¾ cup) water. Cover the pan and cook over high heat for 1–2 minutes, or until they open (discard any that stay closed after that time). Drain, reserving the liquid. Remove the clams from their shells and set aside.

2 Clean the octopus by slitting the head and pulling out the innards. Cut out the eyes and hard beak and rinse. Lie the squid out flat, skin side up, and score a crisscross pattern into the flesh, being careful not to cut all the way through. Slice diagonally into 2 x 4 cm (¾ x 1½ inch) strips. Peel and devein the prawns.

3 Score a cross in the top of each tomato, plunge them into boiling water for 20 seconds, then drain and peel the skin away from the cross. Core and chop. Cook the pasta in a large saucepan of boiling salted water until al dente.

4 Meanwhile, heat the oil in a large frying pan and add the garlic and tomato. Stir over moderate heat for 10–15 seconds, then pour in the saffron-infused wine and the reserved clam liquid. Season and simmer for 8–10 minutes, or until reduced by half. Add the squid, prawns and octopus and cook until the squid turns opaque. Add the scallops, clam meat and parsley and cook until the scallops turn opaque.

5 Drain the spaghetti and return to the pan. Add two-thirds of the sauce, toss well then transfer to a large serving platter. Spoon the remaining sauce over the top and serve with fresh lemon wedges.

ORECCHIETTE WITH BROCCOLI AND CHILLI SAUCE

SERVES 4

250 g (9 oz) broccoli

400 g (14 oz) orecchiette

75 ml (2¼ fl oz) extra virgin olive oil

2 garlic cloves, finely chopped

½ large red chilli, finely chopped

1 tablespoon chopped rosemary

25 g (1 oz) parmesan cheese, grated, plus extra to serve

extra virgin olive oil, to serve

1   Bring a large saucepan of salted water to the boil. Cut the broccoli into small florets and add them to the water with the pasta. Cook until the pasta is al dente (the broccoli will be very tender and may have broken up) then drain briefly, reserving a small cup of the water.

2   Heat the olive oil in the saucepan and add the garlic, chilli and rosemary. Cook gently for a couple of minutes until the garlic is light golden brown. Remove from the heat, add the broccoli and pasta and mix well—the broccoli should break up and create the sauce.

3   Add a little of the cooking water to loosen the pasta if necessary, then season well and stir in the parmesan. Serve immediately with a drizzle of olive oil and the extra parmesan.

SERVES 4

200 g (7 oz) shelled walnuts

20 g (¾ oz) roughly chopped flat-leaf (Italian) parsley

1 garlic clove, crushed

50 g (1¾ oz) butter, softened

200 ml (7 fl oz) extra virgin olive oil

30 g (1 oz) parmesan, grated

100 ml (3½ fl oz) thick (double/heavy) cream

400 g (14 oz) tagliatelle or pappardelle

1 Lightly toast the walnuts in a dry frying pan over moderately high heat for about 2 minutes, or until they brown and smell nutty. Set them aside until they are completely cold.

2 Put the walnuts in a food processor with the parsley and garlic and mix until they are finely chopped. If you do not have a processor, use a knife to finely chop the nuts, parsley and garlic. Add the butter and mix together well.

3 With the motor of the processor running, gradually pour in the olive oil in a steady stream. Again, if you do not have a processor, put the nut mixture in a large bowl and add the oil, mixing well. Add the parmesan and the cream. Season with salt.

4 Cook the pasta in a large saucepan of boiling salted water until al dente. Drain briefly, then toss with the walnut sauce to serve.

VINCISGRASSI

SERVES 4

MEAT SAUCE

1 kg (2 lb 4 oz) cotechino sausages, casings removed, chopped
40 g (1½ oz) butter
800 g (1 lb 12 oz) chicken thigh fillets, cut into thin strips
300 g (10½ oz) chicken livers, chopped
75 ml (2¼ fl oz) dry Marsala
200 ml (7 fl oz) chicken stock

MUSHROOM SAUCE

1 onion, finely chopped
40 g (1½ oz) butter
10 g (¼ oz) porcini mushrooms, chopped
100 g (3½ oz) button mushrooms, sliced
pinch of ground nutmeg
1 tablespoon chicken stock

BECHAMEL SAUCE

850 ml (29 fl oz) milk
1 bay leaf
1 small onion
6 garlic cloves
50 g (1¾ oz) unsalted butter
40 g (1½ oz) plain (all-purpose) flour
125 ml (4 fl oz/½ cup) thick cream
½ nutmeg, freshly grated

6 dried lasagne sheets
75 g (2½ oz) parmesan cheese, grated

1 **To make the meat sauce,** fry the sausage in the butter until browned. Add the chicken and chicken liver and fry quickly until browned. Season, add the Marsala and cook until evaporated. Add the stock, cover and cook for 25 minutes. To make the mushroom sauce, cook the onion in the butter until soft. Add the porcini and mushrooms and cook for 2–3 minutes. Season, add the nutmeg and stock and simmer until the liquid evaporates.

2 **To make the béchamel sauce,** put the milk in a saucepan with the bay leaf and the onion studded with the cloves. Bring to the boil, remove from the heat and leave to stand for at least 20 minutes. Melt the butter in another saucepan and mix in the flour to make a roux. Cook over low heat, stirring, for 2 minutes. Remove from the heat, strain the milk and add it to the roux, stirring to prevent lumps. Simmer gently for

10 minutes until the sauce is creamy. Add the cream, season with salt, pepper and nutmeg and pour half into a bowl. Add the mushroom sauce to the other half and mix well.

3 **For the pasta,** boil the sheets briefly and blot dry before use.

4 **Preheat the oven** to 200°C (400°F/Gas 6). Put a layer of pasta in a greased ovenproof dish. Top with half the meat sauce, then half the mushroom sauce. Sprinkle with a third of the parmesan. Repeat the layers, ending with a layer of béchamel and parmesan. Bake for 30 minutes until golden brown.

LASAGNE AL FORNO

SERVES 6

MEAT SAUCE

30 g (1 oz) butter
1 onion, finely chopped
1 small carrot, finely chopped
½ celery stalk, finely chopped
1 garlic clove, crushed
120 g (4 oz) pancetta, sliced
500 g (1 lb 2 oz) minced beef
¼ teaspoon dried oregano
pinch of nutmeg
90 g (3 oz) chicken livers, trimmed and finely chopped
75 ml (2½ fl oz) dry vermouth or dry white wine
350 ml (12 fl oz) beef stock
1 tablespoon tomato purée
2 tablespoons thick (double/heavy) cream
1 egg, beaten

1 quantity béchamel sauce (page 38)
125 ml (4 fl oz/½ cup) thick (double/heavy) cream
100 g (4 oz) fresh lasagne verde or 6 sheets dried lasagne
150 g (5½ oz) mozzarella, grated
60 g (2 oz) Parmesan, grated

1 **To make the meat sauce**, heat the butter in a frying pan and add the chopped vegetables, garlic and pancetta. Cook over moderately low heat for 5—6 minutes, or until softened and lightly golden. Add the minced beef, increase the heat a little and cook for 8 minutes, or until coloured but not browned, stirring to break up the lumps. Add the oregano and nutmeg and season well.

2 **Stir in the chicken livers** and cook until they change colour. Pour in the vermouth, increase the heat and cook until it has evaporated. Add the beef stock and tomato purée and simmer for 2 hours. Add a little hot water, if necessary, during this time to keep the mixture moist, but towards the end let all the liquid be absorbed. Stir in the cream, remove from the heat and leave to cool for 15 minutes. Stir in the egg.

3 **Put the béchamel** in a saucepan, heat gently and stir in the cream. Remove from heat. Cool slightly. Preheat oven to 180°C (350°F/Gas 4). Grease a 22 x 15 x 7 cm ovenproof dish.

4 **If using fresh pasta**, cut it into manageable sheets and cook in batches in a large pan of boiling salted water until al dente. Scoop out each cooked batch and drop into a bowl of cold water. Spread sheets in a single layer on a tea towel, (dish towel) turning once to blot dry. Trim away any torn edges.

5 **Spread half** the meat sauce in the dish. Scatter with half the mozzarella, then cover with a slightly overlapping layer of pasta sheets. Spread half the béchamel over this and sprinkle with half the Parmesan. Repeat the layers, finishing with a layer of béchamel and Parmesan.

6 **Bake for about 40 minutes** until golden brown and leave to rest for 10 minutes before serving.

ARTICHOKE AND SPINACH CANNELLONI

SERVES 6

FILLING

3 tablespoons olive oil

2 large artichoke hearts, peeled, quartered and thinly sliced or

375 g (13 oz) cleaned hearts

1 onion, thinly sliced

2 garlic cloves, thinly sliced

1 teaspoon finely chopped rosemary

100 ml (3½ fl oz) dry white vermouth or wine

250 g (9 oz) spinach, washed and drained

425 ml (15 fl oz) thick (double/heavy) cream

75 g (2½ oz) parmesan cheese, grated

½ teaspoon freshly grated nutmeg

250 g (9 oz) dried lasagne sheets

butter, for greasing

1 To make the filling, pour the olive oil into a large saucepan or frying pan and cook the artichokes and onion over medium-high heat for 5 minutes, seasoning with salt and pepper. Stir to prevent burning. Add the garlic and rosemary and cook for another few minutes. Add the vermouth and 100 ml (3½ fl oz) water and reduce the liquid into the artichokes until they are softened. Add the spinach, stirring until it is wilted. (If the spinach is large leafed, remove from the heat and use a pair of scissors to coarsely cut it up in the pan.) Add 300 ml (10½ fl oz) of the cream and bring to the boil. Boil briefly, then remove from the heat, add half the parmesan and the nutmeg and check the seasoning.

2 To cook the pasta, bring a saucepan of salted water to the boil and add a dash of oil. This prevents the pasta sheets from sticking to each other but will not affect the filling later. Blanch the pasta for 5 minutes, then drop it into a bowl of cold water.

Spread the sheets out in a single layer on a tea towel (dish towel), turning them over once to blot dry each side. Trim away any torn edges.

3 To assemble the cannelloni, preheat the oven to 180°C (350°F/Gas 4). Butter a rectangular or square 2.5 litre (85 fl oz/10 cup) capacity dish (use one about 20 x 26 cm/ 8 x 10½ inches). Lay out the sheets of pasta on the work surface (work quickly so they don't stick) and divide the filling among them. Spread out the filling and roll each sheet into a fat tube. Put the tubes side by side in the dish, seam side down. Pour over the remaining cream, sprinkle parmesan on top and season.

4 Place the dish on a tray to catch any drips if the cream bubbles over. Bake for 30 minutes or until the top is golden brown. Remove from the oven and leave to cool for 10 minutes before serving.

TORTELLINI FILLED WITH PUMPKIN AND SAGE

SERVES 4

FILLING

900 g (2 lb) pumpkin or butternut squash, peeled and cubed

6 tablespoons olive oil

1 small red onion, finely chopped

100 g (3½ oz) ricotta cheese

1 egg yolk, beaten

25 g (1 oz) parmesan cheese, grated

1 teaspoon freshly grated nutmeg

2 tablespoons chopped sage

1 quantity fresh pasta dough (page 156)

1 egg

2 teaspoons milk

extra virgin olive oil, to serve

grated parmesan cheese, to serve

1 **Preheat the oven** to 190°C (375°F/Gas 5). To make the filling, put the pumpkin in a roasting tin with half the olive oil and lots of salt and pepper. Bake in the oven for 40 minutes, or until it is completely soft.

2 **Meanwhile, heat the remaining olive oil** in a saucepan and gently cook the onion until soft. Put the onion and pumpkin in a bowl, draining off any excess oil, and mash well. Leave to cool, then crumble in the ricotta. Mix in the egg yolk, parmesan, nutmeg and sage. Season well.

3 **To make the tortellini,** roll out the pasta to the thinnest setting on the machine or with a large rolling pin. Cut the pasta into 8 cm (3¼ inch) squares. Mix together the egg and milk to make an egg wash and brush lightly over the pasta just before you fill each one.

4 **To fill the pasta,** put a small teaspoon of filling in the middle of each square and fold it over diagonally to make a triangle, pressing down the corners. Pinch together the two corners on the longer side. If you are not cooking the tortellini immediately, place them, well spaced out, on baking paper dusted with semolina and cover with a tea towel (dish towel). They can be left for 1–2 hours, but don't refrigerate or they will become damp.

5 **Cook the tortellini** in small batches in a large saucepan of boiling salted water until al dente. Remove with a slotted spoon and allow to drain. Serve with a drizzle of olive oil and grated parmesan.

TORTELLINI FILLED WITH WILD MUSHROOMS

SERVES 4

FILLING

50 g (1¾ oz) dried wild mushrooms
  such as porcini

50 g (1¾ oz) butter

2 small garlic cloves, finely chopped

2 teaspoons chopped thyme

250 g (9 oz) ricotta cheese

50 g (1¾ oz) parmesan cheese, grated

1 quantity fresh pasta dough (page 156)

1 egg

2 teaspoons milk

extra virgin olive oil, to serve

grated parmesan cheese, to serve

1 To make the filling, put the mushrooms in just enough hot water to cover them and leave to soak for 15 minutes. Remove the mushrooms, reserving the soaking liquid, and coarsely chop them.

2 Melt the butter in a saucepan and add the mushrooms. Gently cook for a few minutes, season, then add the garlic and half the thyme. Cook for a few minutes, making sure the garlic does not burn, then add the soaking liquid.

3 Increase the heat and cook for about 5 minutes or until the liquid thickens and coats the mushrooms. Using a spatula, scrape the mushrooms and the reduced liquid into a bowl and leave to cool. Add the ricotta, parmesan and the remaining thyme and season well with salt and pepper.

4 To make the tortellini, roll out the pasta to the thinnest setting on the machine or with a large rolling pin. Cut the pasta into 8 cm (3¼ inch) squares. Mix together the egg and milk and brush lightly over the pasta just before you fill each one. To fill the pasta, put a small teaspoon of filling in the middle of each square and fold it over diagonally to make a triangle, pressing down the corners. Pinch together the two corners on the longer side. If you are not cooking the tortellini immediately, place them, well spaced out, on baking paper dusted with semolina and cover with a tea towel (dish towel). They can be left for 1–2 hours, but don't refrigerate or they will become damp.

5 Cook the tortellini in small batches in a large saucepan of boiling salted water until al dente. Remove with a slotted spoon and allow to drain. Serve with a drizzle of olive oil and grated parmesan.

SARDINIAN RAVIOLI

SERVES 4

FILLING

4 tablespoons mixed fresh herbs such as flat-leaf (Italian) parsley, basil, mint, marjoram, oregano and thyme, chopped
250 g (9 oz) ricotta cheese
250 g (9 oz) pecorino cheese, grated
1 egg
pinch of freshly grated nutmeg
1 quantity fresh pasta dough (page 156)
1 egg
2 teaspoons milk
tomato sauce (see page 25)

1 **To make the filling,** mix the herbs with the ricotta, pecorino, egg and nutmeg. Season.

2 **To make the ravioli,** roll out the pasta dough to the thinnest setting of the machine or with a rolling pin. Don't roll out more than you can handle at a time.

3 **Cut circles out** of the dough with a 9 cm (3½ inch) round cutter or an upturned wine glass. Mix together the egg and milk and brush over each circle just before filling.

4 **Place 2 teaspoons of the filling** in the centre of each circle. Fold over the top of the circle to make a half-moon shape. Use your finger to press down around the filling to remove any air pockets. Run your finger firmly around the edge to seal well.

5 **Put the ravioli,** well spaced out, on a tray dusted with semolina and leave to dry for a few minutes before cooking. The ravioli can be cooked immediately or left for up to 1 hour.

6 **Cook the ravioli** in batches in a large saucepan of boiling salted water until al dente. Remove with a slotted spoon and rest the spoon on a tea towel (dish towel) to drain away any remaining water.

7 **Serve** with a tomato sauce and some grated pecorino, or on its own with melted unsalted butter.

PIZZOCCHERI

SERVES 4

PIZZOCCHERI

200 g (7 oz) buckwheat flour

100 g (3½ oz) plain bread flour

1 egg

120 ml (4 fl oz) milk, warmed

CABBAGE, POTATO AND CHEESE SAUCE

350 g (12 oz) savoy cabbage, roughly chopped

180 g (6 oz) potatoes, cut into 2 cm (¾ inch) cubes

4 tablespoons extra virgin olive oil

1 small bunch sage, finely chopped

2 garlic cloves, finely chopped

350 g (12 oz) mixed cheeses (mascarpone, fontina, taleggio and gorgonzola), cubed

grated parmesan cheese, to serve

1   To make the pizzoccheri, sift the two flours into a bowl and add a pinch of salt. Make a well in the centre and add the egg. Mix the egg into the flour and then gradually add the milk, mixing continuously until you have a soft dough. You may find that you need more or less milk than specified.

2   Knead the dough for a few minutes, or until it is elastic, and then cover and leave to rest for an hour. Using a pasta machine or rolling pin, roll out the dough very thinly and cut into ribbons about 1 cm (½ inch) wide.

3   To make the sauce, bring a large saucepan of salted water to the boil. Add the cabbage and potato and cook for about 3–5 minutes, or until cooked through, and then add the pasta for the last 2 minutes of cooking. (If you are using ready-made dried pasta, cook the pasta, cabbage and potatoes together for about 5–8 minutes, or until they are all cooked.)

4   Drain the pasta, cabbage and potatoes, reserving a cup of the cooking water. Dry the saucepan, then add the olive oil and gently cook the sage and garlic for 1 minute. Add the mixed cheeses to the pan. Mix briefly, then add the pasta, cabbage and potatoes and season with salt and pepper.

5   Remove the saucepan from the heat and gently stir the mixture together, adding some pasta water to loosen it up a little if necessary. Serve with parmesan sprinkled over the top.

POTATO GNOCCHI WITH PANCETTA AND BASIL

SERVES 4

POTATO GNOCCHI

1 kg (2 lb 4 oz) floury potatoes, unpeeled
2 egg yolks
2 tablespoons grated parmesan cheese
125–185 g (4½–6½ oz) plain (all-purpose) flour

SAUCE

75 g (2½ oz) pancetta
50 g (1¾ oz) butter
handful of basil leaves, torn

1 **Prick the potatoes** all over and bake for 1 hour, or until tender. Cool for 15 minutes, then peel and mash (do not use a food processor or the potatoes will become gluey).

2 **Mix in the yolks** and parmesan, then gradually stir in the flour. When the mixture gets too dry to use a spoon, use your hands. Once a loose dough forms, transfer to a lightly floured surface and knead gently. Work in enough extra flour to give a very soft, light, pliable dough.

3 **Divide the dough** into six portions. Dust your hands lightly in flour, then, working with one portion at a time, roll out on a floured surface to make a rope about 1.5 cm (5/8 inch) thick. Cut into 1.5 cm (5/8 inch) lengths. Take each piece of dough and press your finger into it to form a concave shape, then roll the outer surface over the tines of a fork to make deep ridges. Fold the outer lips in towards each other to make a hollow

in the middle. Place on a lightly floured tray and leave to rest, ideally for 10 minutes or more.

4 **To make the sauce,** fry the pancetta in the butter until crisp and set aside.

5 **Bring a large saucepan** of salted water to the boil, then reduce the heat a little. Add the gnocchi in batches, stir gently and return to the boil. Cook until they rise to the surface. Remove with a slotted spoon and drain. Add the basil to the pancetta and toss together, season well and sprinkle over the gnocchi.

SPINACH AND RICOTTA GNOCCHI WITH SAGE BUTTER

SERVES 4

GNOCCHI

1.5 kg (3 lb 5 oz) fresh spinach, stalks removed, or 400 g (14 oz) thawed frozen spinach

50 g (1¾ oz) butter

1 onion, finely chopped

1 garlic clove, finely chopped

1 tablespoon chopped marjoram leaves

1 small nutmeg, grated

250 g (9 oz) ricotta cheese

2 eggs

75 g (2½ oz) plain (all-purpose) flour, plus extra for dusting

50 g (1¾ oz) fresh breadcrumbs

100 g (3½ oz) parmesan cheese, grated

SAGE BUTTER

75 g (2½ oz) butter

15 g (½ oz) sage, stems removed

grated parmesan cheese, to serve

1 **To make the gnocchi,** cook the spinach in a large saucepan with a generous amount of salt and a little water until it just begins to wilt. Drain, then rinse in cold water and squeeze as dry as possible. Finely chop.

2 **Melt the butter** and cook the onion and garlic until soft and translucent. Add the marjoram, spinach and nutmeg and season. Remove from the heat, put the spinach in a large bowl and spread it out to cool completely.

3 **Stir in the ricotta,** eggs, flour, breadcrumbs and parmesan. Taste for seasoning and add more salt, pepper or parmesan, if needed. The gnocchi should be well seasoned as they will be dusted with flour and then cooked in water, which tends to dilute their flavour a little. Put the mixture in the fridge and allow it to chill and stiffen up.

4 **Roll the gnocchi** into walnut-sized balls, dusting your hands regularly with flour as the mixture will be sticky, and put them on a lightly floured tray. This might be a little messy, so occasionally rinse your hands in warm water.

5 **To make the sage butter,** melt the butter and stir in the sage.

6 **Bring a large saucepan** of salted water to the boil, then reduce the heat a little. Add the gnocchi in batches, stir gently and return to the boil. Don't overcrowd the saucepan with the gnocchi or they might break up. Cook until they rise to the surface. Remove with a slotted spoon and drain. Once they are cooked, pour on the sage butter and sprinkle with parmesan.

ROMAN GNOCCHI

SERVES 4

45 g (1½ oz) unsalted butter, melted

30 g (1 oz) parmesan cheese, grated

3 egg yolks

1 litre (35 fl oz/4 cups) milk

pinch of freshly grated nutmeg

200 g (7 oz) semolina

TOPPING

40 g (1½ oz) butter, melted

90 ml (3 fl oz) thick (double/heavy) cream (optional)

30 g (1 oz) parmesan cheese, grated

1 Line a 25 x 30 cm (10 x 12 inch) shallow baking tin with baking paper, leaving some overhang on each side. Beat the butter, parmesan and egg yolks and season lightly.

2 Heat the milk in a large saucepan and season with salt, pepper and the nutmeg. When the milk is just boiling, pour in the semolina in a steady stream, stirring constantly. Reduce the heat and continue to cook, stirring, for about 10–12 minutes, or until all the milk has been absorbed and the mixture pulls away from the side of the pan in one lump.

3 Remove the saucepan from the heat and beat in the egg yolk mixture with a wooden spoon until smooth. Spoon quickly into the tin (if you take too long, the mixture will begin to stiffen). Smooth the surface with a knife dipped in cold water. Set aside to cool.

4 Preheat the oven to 180°C (350°F/Gas 4) and grease a 18 x 25 cm (7 x 10 inch) shallow casserole or baking tray. Lift the semolina slab out of the tin and peel off the baking paper. Cut the semolina into circles, using a 4 cm (½ inch) biscuit cutter dipped in cold water. If you don't have a cutter, use an upturned glass instead. Arrange the circles, slightly overlapping, in the greased casserole.

5 To make the topping, blend the butter and cream (if using). Pour this over the gnocchi and sprinkle the parmesan on top. If you are using just butter, simply dot it over the top. Bake for about 25–30 minutes, or until golden. Serve at once.

RICE & POLENTA

RISOTTO MILANESE

SERVES 4

200 ml (7 fl oz) dry white vermouth or white wine

1 large pinch of saffron strands

1.5 litres (52 fl oz/6 cups) chicken stock

100 g (3½ oz) butter

75 g (2½ oz) beef marrow

1 large onion, finely chopped

1 garlic clove, crushed

350 g (12 oz) risotto rice

150 g (5½ oz) parmesan cheese, grated

1 Put the vermouth or wine in a bowl, add the saffron and leave to soak for 10 minutes. Heat the chicken stock in a saucepan and maintain at a low simmer.

2 Melt the butter and beef marrow in a deep heavy-based frying pan and gently cook the onion and garlic until soft but not browned. Add the rice and reduce the heat to low. Season and stir to coat the grains of rice in the butter and marrow.

3 Add the vermouth and saffron to the rice and increase the heat to medium. Cook, stirring, until all the liquid has been absorbed.

4 Stir in a ladleful of the stock and cook at a fast simmer, stirring constantly. When the stock has been absorbed, stir in another ladleful. Continue like this for about 20 minutes, or until the rice is al dente. Add a little more stock or water if you need to—every risotto will use a different amount.

5 Stir in 100 g (3½ oz) of the parmesan and sprinkle the rest over the top to serve.

FENNEL AND SEAFOOD RISOTTO

SERVES 4

250 g (9 oz) large prawns (shrimp)
300 ml (10½ oz) dry white vermouth or white wine
700 ml (24 fl oz) fish stock
100 g (3½ oz) butter
1 onion, finely chopped
2 small heads of fennel, cubed
1 garlic clove, finely chopped
200 g (7 oz) risotto rice
20 g (¾ oz) flat-leaf (Italian) parsley, roughly chopped

1   Peel and devein the prawns and put the shells and heads in a saucepan with the vermouth and fish stock. Bring to the boil and simmer for 10 minutes. Strain the liquid into a jug—you should have about 750 ml (26 fl oz/3 cups)—then return to the pan and maintain at a low simmer.

2   Melt the butter in a deep heavy-based frying pan and gently cook the onion until soft but not browned. Add the fennel and garlic and cook for 5 minutes, stirring occasionally to prevent sticking. Add the rice and reduce the heat to low. Season and stir to coat the grains of rice in the butter.

3   Stir in a ladleful of the stock and cook at a fast simmer, stirring constantly. When the stock has been absorbed, stir in another ladleful. Continue like this for about 20 minutes, or until the rice is al dente. When you have added three-quarters of the stock, add the prawns. Add a little more stock or water if you need to—every risotto will use a different amount—until the prawns are pink and cooked and the rice is al dente. Stir in the parsley.

RISOTTO NERO

SERVES 4

3 squid

1 litre (35 fl oz/4 cups) fish stock

100 g (3½ oz) butter

1 red onion, finely chopped

2 garlic cloves, crushed

350 g (12 oz) risotto rice

3 sachets of squid or cuttlefish ink or the
   ink sacs of the squid

150 ml (5 fl oz) white wine

2 teaspoons olive oil

1   Prepare the squid by pulling the heads and tentacles out of the bodies along with any innards. Cut the heads off below the eyes, leaving just the tentacles. Discard the heads and set the tentacles aside. Rinse the tentacles and bodies, pulling out the transparent quills. Pull the skin off the tentacles and bodies. Finely chop the bodies and cut the tentacles in half.heat the fish stock in a saucepan and maintain at a low simmer.

2   Heat the butter in a deep heavy-based frying pan and cook the onion until softened but not browned. Increase the heat and add the squid bodies. Cook for 3 minutes, or until opaque. Add the garlic and stir briefly. Add the rice and reduce the heat to low. Season and stir to coat the grains of rice in the butter.

3   Squeeze the ink from the sachets and add with the wine. Increase the heat and stir until absorbed.

4   Stir in a ladleful of the stock and cook at a fast simmer, stirring constantly. When the stock has been absorbed, stir in another ladleful. Continue like this for about 20 minutes, or until the rice is al dente. Add a little more stock or water if you need to—every risotto will use a different amount.

5   Heat the olive oil in a frying pan and fry the squid tentacles quickly. Use to garnish the risotto.

PORCINI RISOTTO

SERVES 4

30 g (1 oz) dried porcini mushrooms

1 litre (35 fl oz/4 cups) chicken or
    vegetable stock

100 g (3½ oz) butter

1 onion, finely chopped

250 g (9 oz) mushrooms, sliced

2 garlic cloves, crushed

375 g (13 oz) risotto rice

pinch of ground nutmeg

1 tablespoon finely chopped parsley

45 g (1½ oz) parmesan cheese, grated

1 **Put the porcini in a bowl,** cover with 500 ml (17 fl oz/
2 cups) hot water and leave to soak for 15 minutes. Squeeze
them dry, reserving the soaking liquid. If the porcini are large,
roughly chop them. Strain the soaking liquid into a saucepan
and add enough stock to make up to 1 litre (35 fl oz/4 cups).
Heat up and maintain at a low simmer.

2 **Melt the butter** in a deep heavy-based frying pan and
gently cook the onion until soft but not browned. Add the
mushrooms and porcini and fry for a few minutes. Add the
garlic, stir briefly, then add the rice and reduce the heat to low.
Season and stir to coat the grains of rice in the butter.

3 **Increase the heat** to medium and add a ladleful of the
stock. Cook at a fast simmer, stirring constantly. When the
stock has been absorbed, stir in another ladleful. Continue
like this for about 20 minutes, or until the rice is al dente. Add
a little more stock or water if you need to—every risotto will
use a different amount.

4 **Stir in the nutmeg,** parsley and half the parmesan, then
serve with the rest of the parmesan sprinkled over the top.

ASPARAGUS RISOTTO

SERVES 4

450 g (1 lb) asparagus
100 g (3½ oz) butter
1 onion, finely chopped
1 large garlic clove, finely chopped
1 tablespoon chopped thyme
225 g (8 oz) risotto rice
150 ml (5 fl oz) dry white vermouth or white wine
25 g (1 oz) parmesan cheese, grated, plus shavings to serve

1   To make the stock, wash the asparagus and snap off the woody ends but don't throw them away. Cut the tips off the asparagus and set aside. Finely chop the asparagus stems.

2   Pour 750 ml (26 fl oz/3 cups) water into a small saucepan, add a pinch of salt and bring to the boil. Cook the woody asparagus ends in the water for about 10 minutes. Remove the ends with the spoon and throw them away. In the same water, cook the asparagus tips for 2 minutes, then remove, drain and set aside. Finally, cook the chopped asparagus stems for 3 minutes.

3   Pour the water and asparagus stems into a blender and mix until smooth. Pour into a measuring jug—you should have 750 ml (26 fl oz/3 cups) of liquid. Pour the stock back into the saucepan and maintain at a low simmer.

4   Heat 75 g (2½ oz) of the butter in deep heavy-based frying pan and gently cook the onion until soft but not browned.

Add the garlic and thyme and stir. Add the rice and reduce the heat to low. Season and stir to coat.

5   Add the vermouth to the rice and increase the heat to medium. Cook, stirring, until all the liquid has been absorbed.

6   Stir in a ladleful of the stock and cook at a fast simmer, stirring constantly. When the stock has been absorbed, stir in another ladleful. Continue like this for about 20 minutes, or until the rice is al dente. When you have one ladleful of stock left, add the asparagus tips and the remaining stock and cook until the liquid is absorbed. Adding the delicate asparagus tips at the end of cooking prevents them breaking up and helps them maintain their bright green colour.

7   Stir in the remaining butter and parmesan. Leave the risotto in the pan for 1–2 minutes to allow the flavours to infuse. Sprinkle with the remaining parmesan to serve.

SERVES 4

500 ml (17 fl oz/2 cups) chicken stock
1 thyme sprig
100 g (3½ oz) butter
1 onion, finely chopped
1 large garlic clove, finely chopped
225 g (8 oz) risotto rice
500 ml (17 fl oz/2 cups) dry red wine
25 g (1 oz) parmesan cheese, grated, plus extra to serve

1 **Heat the chicken stock** in a saucepan and maintain at a low simmer.

2 **Strip the leaves** from the thyme sprig.

3 **Melt the butter** in a deep heavy-based frying pan and gently cook the onion and garlic until soft but not browned. Add the thyme and rice and reduce the heat to low. Season and stir to coat the grains of rice in the butter.

4 **Add half the red wine** to the rice and increase the heat to medium. Cook, stirring, until all the liquid has been absorbed. Stir in half the stock and cook at a fast simmer, stirring constantly. When the stock has been absorbed, stir in the rest of the wine.

5 **Stir in nearly all the rest of the stock** and cook until the rice is al dente. Add a little more stock or water if you need to—every risotto will use a different amount.

6 **Stir in the parmesan** and sprinkle a little extra over the top to serve.

RISI E BISI

SERVES 4

1.5 litres (52 fl oz/6 cups) chicken or vegetable stock

100 g (3½ oz) butter

1 large onion, finely chopped

2 garlic cloves, finely chopped

350 g (12 oz) fresh or frozen peas

350 g (12 oz) risotto rice

200 ml (7 fl oz) dry white vermouth or white wine

50 g (1¾ oz) parmesan cheese, grated, plus extra to serve

1 Heat the stock in a saucepan and maintain at a low simmer.

2 Melt 75 g (2½ oz) of the butter in a deep heavy-based frying pan and gently cook the onion and garlic until soft but not browned. If you are using frozen peas, blanch them in the chicken stock for 1 minute, then drain them over a bowl and set aside. Pour this stock back into the saucepan.

3 Add the rice to the frying pan and reduce the heat to low. Season and stir to coat the grains of rice in the butter. Add the vermouth and increase the heat to medium. Cook, stirring, until all the liquid has been absorbed.

4 Stir in a ladleful of the stock and cook at a fast simmer, stirring constantly. When the stock has been absorbed, stir in another ladleful.

5 If you are using fresh peas, add them after the first couple of ladles of stock. If using frozen blanched peas, add them after half the stock has been used. Continue adding a ladleful of stock at a time for about 20 minutes, or until the rice is al dente. Add a little more stock or water if you need to—every risotto will use a different amount. The consistency of this dish should be like a thick soup or wet risotto.

6 Remove the risotto from the heat and leave to rest for 5 minutes, then stir in the remaining butter and the parmesan. Serve with extra parmesan.

SPINACH RISOTTO CAKE

SERVES 4

250 g (9 oz) baby spinach
750 ml (26 fl oz/3 cups) chicken stock
100 g (3½ oz) butter
1 onion, finely chopped
1 garlic clove, finely chopped
225 g (8 oz) arborio rice
150 ml (5 fl oz) dry white vermouth or white wine
¼ teaspoon freshly grated nutmeg
25 g (1 oz) parmesan cheese, grated, plus extra to serve

1 **Cook the spinach** in a small amount of salted water until just wilted. Refresh in cold water and squeeze dry. Finely chop and set aside.

2 **Heat the chicken** stock in a saucepan and maintain at a low simmer.

3 **Melt** 75 g (2½ oz) of the butter in a deep heavy-based frying pan and gently cook the onion and garlic until soft but not browned. Add the rice and reduce the heat to low. Season and stir to coat the grains of rice in the butter.

4 **Add the vermouth** to the rice and increase the heat to medium. Cook, stirring, until all the liquid has been absorbed.

5 **Stir in a ladleful** of the stock and cook at a fast simmer, stirring constantly. When the stock has been absorbed, stir in another ladleful. Continue like this until a quarter of the stock is left, then mix in the chopped spinach. Continue to add the last of the stock. When making risotto cake, it is not so essential to keep the rice al dente—if it is a little more glutinous, it will stick together better. Make sure all the liquid is absorbed or the cake may break up when unmoulded. Remove from the heat and stir in the nutmeg, parmesan and the remaining butter.

6 **Smear a little butter** into a mould such as a 1.25-litre (44 fl oz/5 cup) cake tin. Spoon the risotto into the mould, pressing it down firmly. Leave to rest for 5 minutes, then unmould and place on a warm serving plate with some parmesan sprinkled over the top.

ARANCINI

SERVES 4

large pinch of saffron strands

250 ml (9 fl oz/1 cup) white wine

750 ml (26 fl oz/3 cups) chicken stock

2 thyme sprigs

100 g (3½ oz) butter

1 onion, finely chopped

1 garlic clove, finely chopped

225 g (8 oz) risotto rice

50 g (1¾ oz) parmesan cheese, grated

100 g (3½ oz) mozzarella or fontina, diced

75 g (2½ oz) plain (all-purpose) flour

2 eggs, beaten

75 g (2½ oz) dried breadcrumbs

500 ml (17 fl oz/2 cups) oil, for deep-frying

1 **Put the saffron** in a bowl with the white wine and soak for 10 minutes. Heat the chicken stock in a saucepan and simmer. Strip the leaves from the thyme sprigs.

2 **Melt the butter** in a deep heavy-based frying pan and gently cook the onion and garlic until soft but not browned. Add the thyme and rice and reduce the heat to low. Season and stir to coat the grains of rice in the butter.

3 **Add the wine** and saffron to the rice and increase the heat to medium. Cook, stirring, until all the liquid has been absorbed. Stir in a ladleful of the stock and cook at a fast simmer, stirring constantly. When the stock has been absorbed, stir in another ladleful. Continue like this for about 20 minutes. Add a little more stock or water if you need to—every risotto will use a different amount. When making arancini, it is not so essential to keep the rice al dente—if it

is a little more glutinous, the balls will stick together better. Make sure the risotto is thick or the arancini may break up.

4 **Remove from the heat,** stir in the parmesan, then spread out on a tray lined with greaseproof paper. Leave in the fridge for a couple of hours or overnight to allow the butter and the starch in the rice to solidify. Roll a small amount of risotto into a walnut-sized ball. Press a hollow in the middle with your thumb, insert a small cube of cheese in the hole and firmly press the rice back into place around the cheese. Roll in the flour, then the egg and then in the breadcrumbs.

5 **Heat the oil** in a deep frying pan to 180°C (350°F), or until a piece of bread fries golden brown in 15 seconds. If the oil starts to smoke, it is too hot. Deep-fry the arancini in batches for about 3–4 minutes, making sure they cook evenly on all sides. Drain on paper towels and serve hot or at room temperature.

WET POLENTA WITH MUSHROOMS

SERVES 4

1 tablespoon salt
300 g (10½ oz) fine polenta
3 tablespoons olive oil
400 g (14 oz) wild mushrooms, such as fresh porcini, sliced if large
2 garlic cloves, crushed
1 tablespoon chopped thyme
150 g (5½ oz) mascarpone
50 g (1¾ oz) butter
50 g (1¾ oz) parmesan cheese, grated, plus extra to serve

1 **Bring** 1.5 litres (52 fl oz/6 cups) of water to the boil in a deep heavy-based saucepan and add the salt. Add the polenta in a gentle stream, whisking or stirring vigorously as you pour. Reduce the heat immediately so the water is simmering and keep stirring for the first 30 seconds to prevent lumps appearing—the more you stir, the better the finished texture of the polenta. Leave the polenta to gently bubble away for about 40 minutes, stirring it every few minutes to stop it sticking to the pan. The finished polenta should drop from the spoon in thick lumps.

2 **While the polenta is cooking,** heat the olive oil in a largefrying pan, then add enough mushrooms to cover the base of the pan. Cook over high heat, stirring frequently, until any liquid given off by the mushrooms has evaporated.

3 **Add the garlic** and thyme and cook briefly. Remove the mushrooms from the pan and cook the next batch. Return all mushrooms to the pan and season well.

4 **When the polenta** is almost cooked, reheat the mushrooms, add the mascarpone and let it melt.

5 **Add the butter** and parmesan to the cooked polenta and season with pepper. Spoon the polenta onto plates and top with the mushroom mixture. Sprinkle with extra parmesan to serve.

GRILLED POLENTA WITH SAUSAGE AND TOMATO SAUCE

SERVES 4

POLENTA

1 tablespoon salt

300 g (10½ oz) coarse-grain polenta

50 g (1¾ oz) butter

50 g (1¾ oz) parmesan cheese, grated, plus extra to serve

SAUSAGE AND TOMATO SAUCE

3 tablespoons olive oil

8 firm Italian pork sausages

1 onion, halved and sliced

2 garlic cloves, chopped,

200 ml (7 fl oz) red wine

400 g (14 oz) tinned tomatoes

1 Bring 1.5 litres (52 fl oz/6 cups) of water to the boil in a deep heavy-based saucepan and add the salt. Add the polenta in a gentle stream, whisking or stirring vigorously as you pour. Reduce the heat immediately so the water is simmering and keep stirring for the first 30 seconds to prevent lumps appearing—the more you stir, the better the finished texture of the polenta. Leave the polenta to gently bubble away for about 40 minutes, stirring it every few minutes to stop it sticking to the pan. The finished polenta should drop from the spoon in thick lumps. Stir in the butter and parmesan.

2 Pour the polenta onto a flat plate or serving dish and leave to cool at room temperature.

3 To make the sauce, heat the olive oil in a deep frying pan and cook the sausages over medium-high heat, lightly browning on all sides. Remove the sausages and set aside. Add

the onion and cook gently until softened, scraping the dark brown sausage fat from the bottom of the pan. This will help darken the sauce and improve its flavour.

4 Add the garlic, cook for a few more minutes, then pour in the red wine. Cook for about 5 minutes, or until the liquid has reduced and the sauce thickened. Add the tomatoes and, when the sauce starts to thicken, add the sausages, stirring frequently to prevent the base of the pan from burning. Season with salt and pepper.

5 When the sauce is nearly ready, preheat a chargrill pan or barbecue grill. Cut the polenta into triangles or strips, brush with olive oil and grill for about 3 minutes on each side. Spoon tomato sauce over the sausage and sprinkle the polenta with grated parmesan to serve.

BAKED POLENTA WITH FOUR CHEESES

SERVES 4

POLENTA
1 tablespoon salt

300 g (10½ oz) polenta

75 g (2½ oz) butter

TOMATO SAUCE
2 rosemary or thyme sprigs

3 tablespoons extra virgin olive oil

2 garlic cloves, thinly sliced

800 g (1 lb 12 oz) tinned tomatoes or 350 g (12 oz) ripe tomatoes, peeled and chopped

200 g (7 oz) gorgonzola, cubed

250 g (9 oz) taleggio, cubed

250 g (9 oz) mascarpone

100 g (3½ oz) parmesan cheese, grated

1 Bring 1.5 litres (52 fl oz/6 cups) of water to the boil in a deep heavy-based saucepan and add the salt. Add the polenta in a gentle stream, whisking or stirring vigorously as you pour. Reduce the heat immediately so the water is simmering and keep stirring for the first 30 seconds to prevent lumps appearing—the more you stir, the better the finished texture of the polenta. Leave the polenta to gently bubble away for about 40 minutes, stirring every few minutes. The finished polenta should drop from the spoon in thick lumps. Stir in the butter.

2 Pour the polenta into a large 2.25-litre (76 fl oz/9 cups) oiled gratin or casserole dish that is about 5.5 cm (2¼ inches) deep. The polenta should reach no further than halfway up the side of the dish or the filling will overflow. Leave to cool.

3 To make the tomato sauce, first strip the leaves off the rosemary or thyme. Heat the olive oil in a saucepan over low heat and cook the garlic gently until light brown. Add half the rosemary or thyme and then the tomatoes. Season and cook gently, stirring occasionally, until reduced to a thick sauce.

4 Preheat the oven to 175°C (350°F/Gas 4). Carefully turn the polenta out of the dish onto a board, then slice it horizontally in two. Pour half of the tomato sauce into the bottom of the dish, place the bottom slice of the polenta on top of the sauce and season with salt and pepper. Scatter the gorgonzola and taleggio over the top. Using a teaspoon, dot the mascarpone over the polenta and then sprinkle with half of the parmesan and the remaining rosemary or thyme. Put the other slice of polenta on top and pour over the last of the tomato sauce. Sprinkle with the remaining parmesan and bake for 40 minutes. Leave to rest for at least 10 minutes before serving.

SEAFOOD

MARINATED ANCHOVIES

SERVES 4

400 g (14 oz) fresh anchovies, filleted

4 tablespoons extra virgin olive oil

3 tablespoons lemon juice

2 garlic cloves, crushed

2 tablespoons finely chopped parsley

2 tablespoons finely chopped basil

1 small red chilli, seeded and chopped

1 Carefully wash the fish under cold water and pat dry with paper towels. Place the fillets, skin side down, in a single layer in a shallow serving dish.

2 Mix the remaining ingredients together with some salt and pepper and pour evenly over the anchovies.

3 Cover the dish with plastic wrap and leave the anchovies to marinate in the fridge for at least 3 hours.

4 Before serving, bring the anchovies back to room temperature so they regain their full flavour.

SICILIAN-STYLE STUFFED SARDINES

SERVES 4

8 sardines or large whitebait, butterflied
2 tablespoons extra virgin olive oil
1 small onion, thinly sliced
1 fennel bulb (about 300 g/10½ oz), thinly sliced
25 g (1 oz) pine nuts
2 tablespoons flat-leaf (Italian) parsley, roughly chopped
10 g (¼ oz) fresh breadcrumbs
1 garlic clove, chopped
2 tablespoons lemon juice
extra virgin olive oil
lemon wedges, to serve

1 Rinse the sardines in cold water, drain on paper towels and place in the fridge until needed. Preheat the oven to 200°C (400°F/Gas 6).

2 To prepare the stuffing, pour the olive oil into a saucepan and add the onion, fennel and pine nuts. Cook over medium heat until soft and light brown, stirring frequently. Mix 1 tablespoon of the parsley with 1 tablespoon of the breadcrumbs and set aside.

3 Add the garlic and remaining breadcrumbs to the fennel mixture and cook for a few minutes to lightly crisp the breadcrumbs. Add the remaining parsley, season and set aside. This mixture can be prepared in advance and left in the fridge, but bring back to room temperature before cooking.

4 Drizzle some olive oil in an ovenproof dish, large enough to fit four butterflied sardines in a single layer. Put four sardines in the dish, skin side down, season, then spread the stuffing over the sardines. Put the remaining four sardines on top, skin side up, positioning them tail to tail like a sandwich. Season again and sprinkle with the mixture of parsley and breadcrumbs. Drizzle with the lemon juice and a little olive oil.

5 Put in the oven and cook for about 10 minutes, depending on the size of the sardines (if the filling is still warm, the sardines will take less time to cook). Serve either hot from the oven or at room temperature, with a wedge of lemon. Serve as a starter or part of an antipasto platter.

OCTOPUS SALAD

SERVES 4

650 g (1 lb 7 oz) baby octopus, cleaned

1 garlic clove

2 tablespoons lemon juice

100 ml (3½ oz) extra virgin olive oil

1 tablespoon chopped mint

1 tablespoon chopped parsley

1 teaspoon Dijon mustard

pinch of cayenne pepper

120 g (4¼ oz) misticanza (mixed salad leaves)

lemon wedges, to serve

1   **If the octopus** seem particularly big (they should be in bite-sized portions) cut them into halves or quarters.

2   **Bring a large saucepan** of water to the boil and add the octopus. Simmer for about 8–10 minutes, or until tender.

3   **Lightly smash the garlic** clove with the flat side of a knife. Make a dressing by mixing together the lemon juice, olive oil, mint, parsley, mustard and cayenne with some salt and pepper. Add the garlic and leave to infuse.

4   **Drain the octopus** well and put in a bowl. Pour the dressing over the top and allow to cool for a few minutes before transferring to the fridge. Chill for at least 3 hours, then arrange the octopus on a bed of misticanza. Bring to room temperature, remove the smashed garlic clove and drizzle a little of the dressing over the top. Serve with lemon wedges to squeeze over.

GARLIC PRAWNS

SERVES 4

3 tablespoons olive oil

80 g (2¾ oz) butter

1 red chilli, finely chopped

6 garlic cloves, crushed

20 large prawns (shrimp), peeled and deveined

3 tablespoons white wine

3 tablespoons chopped parsley

1 Put the olive oil in a large frying pan and add the butter, chilli and garlic. Cook, stirring over low heat for about 3 minutes until the garlic and chilli are fragrant. Do not allow the garlic to brown or it will taste bitter. Add the prawns.

2 Cook the prawns for 3 minutes on one side. By this time they should have turned pink and started to brown a little. Turn the prawns, add the wine and cook a further 4 minutes or until the prawns are completely cooked through.

3 Add the parsley, season well with salt and pepper and toss everything together. Serve with bread to mop up the garlic juices.

GRILLED SWORDFISH WITH ANCHOVY AND CAPER SAUCE

SERVES 4

SAUCE

1 large garlic clove

1 tablespoon capers, rinsed and finely chopped

50 g (1¾ oz) anchovy fillets, finely chopped

1 tablespoon finely chopped rosemary or dried oregano

finely grated zest and juice of ½ lemon

4 tablespoons extra virgin olive oil

1 large tomato, finely chopped

4 swordfish steaks

1 tablespoon extra virgin olive oil

bruschetta, to serve (see page 8)

1   **Put the garlic** in a mortar and pestle with a little salt and crush it, or crush it with some salt on a chopping board using the flat of your knife blade.

2   **To make the sauce,** mix together the garlic, capers, anchovies, rosemary or oregano, lemon zest and juice, oil and tomato. Leave for 10 minutes.

3   **Preheat a griddle** or grill (broiler) to very hot. Using paper towels, pat the swordfish dry and lightly brush with the olive oil. Season with salt and pepper. Sear the swordfish over high heat for about 2 minutes on each side (depending on the thickness of the steaks) or until just cooked. To check if the fish is cooked, gently pull apart the centre of one steak — the flesh should be opaque. (Serve with the cut side underneath.)

4   **If the cooked** swordfish is a little oily, drain it on paper towels, then place on serving plates and drizzle with the sauce. Serve with bruschetta to mop up the sauce.

SERVES 4

400 g (14 oz) potatoes, cut into pieces
1 onion, sliced
4 garlic cloves, sliced
1 bay leaf
800 ml (28 fl oz) milk
200 ml (7 fl oz) dry white vermouth or white wine
450 g (1 lb) salt cod, soaked
4 tablespoons flat-leaf (Italian) parsley, roughly chopped
pinch of ground nutmeg
2 egg yolks
2 tablespoons plain (all-purpose) flour, plus a little extra for dusting
oil, for frying
lemon wedges, to serve

1   **Cook the potatoes** in simmering water for 15-20 minutes or until tender. Drain and mash them, then set aside to cool.

2   **Put the onion**, garlic, bay leaf, milk and vermouth in a saucepan, season with pepper and bring to the boil. Add the salt cod, reduce the heat and simmer, covered, for about 10–15 minutes or until the fish is cooked and flakes away from the skin. Leave in the liquid until cool enough to handle.

3   **Place the fish** on a board and separate the meat from the skin and bones (you should have about 300 g/10½ oz). Put the flaked fish in a bowl and add the potatoes, parsley, nutmeg, egg yolks, flour and a little pepper. Mix all the ingredients together and taste for seasoning—you should not need to add any salt. Put the mixture in the fridge for 15 minutes and then roll into 16 small balls and flatten each one slightly.

4   **Heat the oil** in a frying pan. Dust the fritters with a little flour and fry them in batches for about 2 minutes on each side. Drain on paper towels and serve warm with lemon wedges.

SOLE IN SAOR

SERVES 4

pinch of saffron strands

90 ml (3 fl oz) white or red wine vinegar

200 ml (7 fl oz) extra virgin olive oil

1 red onion, thinly sliced

2 garlic cloves, sliced

1 teaspoon coriander seeds

1 teaspoon black peppercorns

1 small cinnamon stick, roughly broken

1 small teaspoon ground allspice
   (optional)

90 ml (3 fl oz) white or red wine

3 teaspoons sugar

2 tablespoons oregano leaves

2 tablespoons plain (all-purpose) flour

4 x 100 g (3½ oz) sole fillets

1 **Put the saffron in a bowl** with the vinegar and leave to soak. Meanwhile, put half the olive oil in a saucepan and gently cook the onion and garlic until softened, being careful that the garlic does not burn.

2 **Put the coriander** and peppercorns in a mortar and pestle and lightly crush them. If you don't have a mortar and pestle, use the base of a rolling pin. Alternatively, the spices can be added whole, but crushing does help to release their flavour and aroma.

3 **Add the crushed spices** to the saucepan with the cinnamon and allspice (if using). Mix briefly to lightly toast the spices, then add the saffron, vinegar, wine and sugar. Bring to the boil and gently simmer for a couple of minutes. Set aside and add the oregano.

4 **Scatter the flour** over a large plate, season with salt and pepper and mix briefly. Make sure the fish fillets are dry by pressing them between two sheets of paper towel, then dust the fish in the flour and pat lightly to remove any large clumps of flour.

5 **Heat a large frying pan** with the remaining olive oil, then fry the fish on both sides until golden brown and cooked through.

6 **Use a gratin dish** large enough to snugly fit the fish in a single layer and pour half the vinegar mixture into the dish. Add the fish and then the remaining liquid. Leave to marinate for at least 1 hour before serving.

BAKED WHOLE FISH WITH FENNEL

SERVES 4

2 heads of fennel

4 tablespoons extra virgin olive oil

1 onion, chopped

1 garlic clove, crushed

1 whole fish, such as sea bass or
sea bream, gutted and scaled

1 lemon, quartered

2 teaspoons chopped oregano, or
½ teaspoon dried oregano

lemon wedges, to serve

1 **Preheat the oven** to 190°C (375°F/Gas 5) and grease a large shallow ovenproof dish. Finely slice the fennel, keeping the green fronds to use later.

2 **Heat the olive oil** in a large frying pan and gently cook the fennel, onion and garlic for 12–15 minutes until softened but not browned. Season with salt and pepper.

3 **Stuff the fish** with a heaped tablespoon of the fennel mixture and a quarter of the fennel fronds. Brush the skin with a little more extra virgin olive oil, squeeze the lemon over and season well.

4 **Spoon the remainder** of the cooked fennel into the dish and sprinkle with half of the oregano. Arrange the fish on top. Sprinkle the remaining oregano over the fish and cover the dish loosely with foil (if you cover it tightly, the fish will steam). Bake for 25 minutes, or until just cooked through — the flesh should feel flaky and the dorsal fin will pull out easily. Serve with lemon wedges.

TUNA INVOLTINI

SERVES 4

4 x 150 g (5½ oz) tuna steaks

6 tablespoons extra virgin olive oil

1 large onion, quartered and finely sliced

200 g (7 oz) small leaf spinach

100 g (3½ oz) olives, pitted and chopped

50 g (1¾ oz) pine nuts, lightly browned

1 small bunch basil, torn

4 tablespoons dried breadcrumbs

lemon wedges, to serve

1 **Preheat the oven** to 200°C (400°F/Gas 6) and heat up the baking dish you are going to use.

2 **Using a mallet** or rolling pin, beat out the tuna steaks between two sheets of greaseproof paper until about 5 mm (¼ inch) thick. Try to keep the tuna shape as even as possible. Place in the fridge until ready to use.

3 **Heat 4 tablespoons** of the olive oil in a frying pan and cook the onion until soft and translucent. Add the spinach and stir until it is just wilted. (If using large-leaf spinach, remove the large stems and roughly chop before adding.) Stir in the olives, pine nuts and basil. Season.

4 **Place the tuna steaks** on a work surface. Remove the top layer of greaseproof paper. Divide the filling among the tuna steaks and roll them up, tucking the stuffing inside. Peel off the bottom sheet of greaseproof as you roll. Roll the tuna in the breadcrumbs.

5 **Drizzle** 1 tablespoon of olive oil into the hot baking dish and put the tuna seam side down in the dish. Drizzle the rest of the olive oil on top and bake in the oven for about 5 minutes, or until the centres of the rolls are hot (test with a skewer). Remove from the oven and serve either hot or cold with a squeeze of lemon juice on top.

STUFFED SQUID

SERVES 4

TOMATO SAUCE

2 tablespoons extra virgin olive oil

1 garlic clove, thinly sliced

800 g (1 lb 12 oz) tinned chopped
    tomatoes

100 ml (3½ oz) red wine

2 tablespoons chopped flat-leaf (Italian)
    parsley

8 squid (about 600 g/1 lb 5 oz), cleaned

STUFFING

100 ml (3½ oz) olive oil

1 small onion, finely chopped

1 small head of fennel, finely chopped

2 garlic cloves, chopped

75 g (2½ oz) arborio rice

large pinch of saffron strands

½ large red chilli, chopped

150 ml (5 fl oz) white wine

3 tablespoons chopped flat-leaf (Italian)
    parsley

1   To make the sauce, put the olive oil and garlic in a saucepan and fry gently for 1 minute. Add the tomatoes and simmer until some of the liquid has evaporated and the sauce is quite thick. Add the wine and parsley and cook the sauce until it has reduced and thickened. Set aside.

2   Finely chop the squid tentacles and set aside with the bodies.

3   To make the stuffing, heat the oil in a large saucepan and gently cook the onion, fennel and garlic for about 10 minutes or until soft. Add the rice, saffron, chilli and chopped squid tentacles and cook for a few minutes, stirring frequently until the tentacles are opaque. Season, then add the wine and 6 tablespoons of the tomato sauce.

4   Cook, stirring frequently, until the tomato and wine has reduced into the rice. Cook for about 5 minutes or until the

liquid has reduced, then add 125 ml (4 fl oz/½ cup) water and continue cooking until the rice is tender and all the liquid has been absorbed. You may need to add a little more water if the rice absorbs all the liquid and is not quite tender. Add 2 tablespoons parsley and set aside to cool for a few minutes.

5   Stuff the squid with the filling, using a teaspoon to push it down into the bottom of the tubes. Do not overfill the tubes. Seal the tops with cocktail sticks.

6   Put the remaining tomato sauce in a saucepan with 200 ml (7 fl oz) water. Cook for 2 minutes, then add the stuffed squid. Cover the saucepan and simmer gently for 30–45 minutes or until the squid are soft and tender. Don't stir the squid too much when cooking or the filling will fall out.

7   Remove the cocktail sticks and sprinkle with the remaining parsley just before serving.

WHOLE FISH COOKED IN SALT WATER

SERVES 4

1 small bunch of seaweed (or dried seaweed, soaked until pliable)

4-8 tablespoons sea salt

1 kg (2 lb 4 oz) whole fish, such as sea bass or sea bream, scaled, gutted and trimmed

1 small onion, roughly chopped

1 small carrot, roughly chopped

6 black peppercorns

1 small bunch herbs, such as parsley, oregano and basil, or a mixture of all three

1 lemon or 4 tablespoons white wine or vinegar

rocket (arugula) leaves and lemon wedges, to serve

SAFFRON AIOLI

pinch of saffron strands

4 egg yolks

2 garlic cloves, crushed

1 tablespoon lemon juice

400 ml (14 fl oz) extra virgin olive oil

1 **Put the seaweed** on the base of a fish poacher or large saucepan. (If using dried seaweed, soak it first to reconstitute it.) Taste a bit of your seaweed to see how salty it is—if it is very salty then use the lesser amount of salt specified.

2 **Place the fish** on top. Add enough water to cover the fish entirely and add the salt, onion, carrot, peppercorns and herbs. Squeeze the juice from the lemon and add to the pan, then cut the lemon into quarters and add that, or the wine or vinegar.

3 **Bring the water to a gentle simmer,** cover and poach the fish for 10–15 minutes until just cooked (press the flesh to see if it feels flaky or pull the dorsal fin, which will come out easily when the fish is ready). Leave in the water for 10 minutes or cool completely and serve at room temperature.

4 **To make the aïoli,** soak the saffron in 1 tablespoon hot water. Put the egg yolks, garlic and lemon juice in a mortar and pestle or food processor and pound or mix them together. Add the oil, drop by drop, mixing until thick and creamy. Add the saffron and taste for salt.

5 **Remove the fish** from the water, briefly drain on a tea towel (dish towel) and serve on the rocket with the aïoli and lemon wedges.

LIGURIAN FISH STEW

SERVES 4

250 g (9 oz) red mullet or red snapper fillet, bones reserved

250 g (9 oz) cod, halibut or turbot fillet, bones reserved

250 g (9 oz) monkfish fillet or any other firm-fleshed white fish, bones reserved

6 large prawns (shrimp), peeled, shells reserved

1 small onion, chopped

1 carrot, chopped

15 g (¼ oz) flat-leaf (Italian) parsley, roughly chopped, stalks reserved

large pinch of saffron strands

300 ml (10½ fl oz) dry white vermouth or wine

1 red onion, halved and thinly sliced

1 large head of fennel, thinly sliced

6 tablespoons extra virgin olive oil

3 garlic cloves, thinly sliced

800 g (1 lb 12 oz) tinned chopped tomatoes

450 g (1 lb) waxy potatoes, quartered lengthways

450 g (1 lb) mussels, cleaned

crostini (see page 12) to serve

1 Cut all the fish fillets into chunks. To make the fish stock, rinse the fish bones in lots of cold water. Put the prawn shells and fish bones in a saucepan, cover with water and slowly bring to a simmer. Add the onion, carrot and parsley stalks, then simmer gently for about 30 minutes.

2 Strain the stock through a fine colander and measure out 1 litre (35 fl oz/4 cups). Set aside.

3 Put the saffron in a bowl with 200 ml (7 fl oz) of the vermouth or wine and leave to soak. Cook the red onion and fennel in the olive oil for about 5 minutes. Add the garlic and the tomatoes. Bring to the boil and simmer until the sauce has reduced and thickened. Season and add the saffron, vermouth and potatoes. Increase the heat and boil for 5 minutes, then add the fish stock, reduce the heat and simmer for 10 minutes, or until the potatoes are cooked.

4 Bring the remaining 100 ml (3½ fl oz) vermouth to the boil in another saucepan and add the mussels. Cover and cook quickly for about 1 minute, or until the shells have just opened. Pick through the mussels, discarding any that haven't opened. Remove the mussels from their shells and put in a bowl. Pour over the cooking liquid, discarding any sediment left in the bottom of the saucepan.

5 Bring the soup base to the boil and add the prawns and fish. Stir briefly, season with salt and pepper and simmer for about 5 minutes, keeping the heat low. Stir in the mussels with their cooking liquid towards the end to reheat them. Remove from the heat

6 Rest for 10 minutes to allow the flavours to develop. Add the parsley and serve in hot bowls topped with crostini.

POULTRY

POLLO ALLA DIAVOLA

SERVES 4

2 x 900 g (2 lb) chickens, spatchcocked

150 ml (5 fl oz) olive oil

juice of 1 large lemon

2 sage leaves

3–4 very small red chillies, finely
    minced, or 1 teaspoon dried
    chilli flakes

½ white onion

2 garlic cloves

4 tablespoons chopped flat-leaf (Italian)
    parsley

2½ tablespoons softened butter

lemon slices, to serve

1   Place the chickens side by side in a shallow dish.

2   Mix together the olive oil, lemon juice, sage and chilli and season well with salt and pepper. Pour over the chicken, cover and leave to marinate in the fridge for 1 hour, turning once.

3   While the chicken is marinating, chop the onion, garlic, parsley and butter in a blender or food processor until the ingredients are fine and paste-like. (If you want to do this by hand, chop the vegetables and herbs finely and then mix them into the softened butter.) Season with salt and pepper. Preheat the grill (broiler) to its highest setting.

4   Place the chickens skin side down on a grill tray. Position the tray about 10 cm (4 inches) below the heat and grill the chickens for 10 minutes, basting with the marinade once or twice. Turn the chickens and grill, basting occasionally, for another 10–12 minutes, or until the juices run clear when a thigh is pierced to the bone with a skewer.

5   Spread the butter paste over the skin of the chickens. Reduce the heat and grill for about 3 minutes until the coating is lightly browned. Serve hot with the butter from the grill pan poured over the chickens, or cold without the extra butter, accompanied by lemon slices.

QUAILS WRAPPED IN VINE LEAVES

SERVES 4

4 rosemary sprigs

4 quails

2 tablespoons olive oil

4 teaspoons balsamic vinegar

2 teaspoons brown sugar

4 large vine leaves, fresh or preserved

1   **Preheat the oven** to 180°C (350°F/Gas 4). Stuff a sprig of rosemary into each quail and then tie its legs together. Tuck the wings behind its back.

2   **Heat the olive oil** in a frying pan and add the quails. Brown them all over and then add the balsamic vinegar and brown sugar and bubble everything together, coating the quail well. Remove from the heat.

3   **Blanch the vine leaves** in boiling water for 15 seconds and then drain and pat dry with kitchen towels. Wrap one vine leaf around each quail, making sure the seam is at the back of the quail. Put the quail in a roasting tin, seam side down, and cook for 15 minutes.

4   **Check the quails** are cooked by piercing the thickest part of the thigh with a skewer—the juices should run clear.

CHICKEN STUFFED WITH FIGS AND FENNEL

SERVES 4

6 tablespoons olive oil

130 g (4¾ oz) smoked pancetta, diced

1 onion, chopped

1 head of fennel, chopped

1 large potato, cut into 2 cm (¾ inch) cubes

2 garlic cloves, chopped

1 tablespoon chopped rosemary

150 ml (5 fl oz) white wine

zest of 1 large orange

4 ripe figs, chopped

1 x 2 kg (4 lb 8 oz) chicken

1 **To make the stuffing,** heat 4 tablespoons of the oil in a saucepan and brown the pancetta and onion. Add the fennel and potato and cook for another few minutes. Season, add the garlic and rosemary and mix briefly. Add the wine, reduce the heat and cover. Cook for about 15 minutes, or until the wine has reduced into the potato and the potato is cooked.

2 **Remove the saucepan** from the heat and add the orange zest and figs. Set aside to cool if not using immediately.

3 **Preheat the oven** to 250°C (500°F/Gas 7). Season the cavity of the chicken, then fill with the stuffing. If there is any leftover stuffing, add it to the roasting tin 15 minutes before removing the chicken from the oven.

4 **Put the chicken breast side up** in the tin, drizzle over the remaining oil and cook for 15 minutes. Remove the chicken from the oven and turn it over on its front, then cook for another 15 minutes. After this time, remove from the oven again and turn it on its back, reduce the heat to 180°C (350°F/Gas 4), and cook for another 30 minutes.

5 **Check the chicken is cooked** by piercing the thickest part of the thigh with a skewer—the juices should run clear. Alternatively, gently pull away one of the legs from the body to check. Check the stuffing is cooked through by pushing a skewer into the cavity for 3 seconds—the skewer should feel very hot when you pull it out. If it isn't, cover the chicken with foil and cook until it is. Remove from the oven and leave to rest for 10 minutes before serving. Serve with any extra stuffing and pour over any juices.

CHICKEN CACCIATORE

SERVES 4

3 tablespoons olive oil

1 large onion, finely chopped

3 garlic cloves, crushed

1 celery stalk, finely chopped

150 g (5½ oz) pancetta, finely chopped

125 g (4½ oz) button mushrooms, thickly sliced

4 chicken drumsticks

4 chicken thighs

90 ml (3 fl oz) dry vermouth or dry white wine

800 g (1 lb 12 oz) tinned chopped tomatoes

¼ teaspoon sugar

1 oregano sprig, plus 4–5 sprigs, to garnish

1 rosemary sprig

1 bay leaf

1 Heat half the oil in a large casserole. Add the onion, garlic, celery and pancetta and cook, stirring occasionally, over low heat for 6–8 minutes, or until the onion is soft and golden.

2 Add the mushrooms, increase the heat and cook, stirring occasionally, for 4–5 minutes. Spoon out onto a plate and set aside.

3 Add the remaining olive oil to the casserole and lightly brown the chicken pieces, a few at a time. Season them as they brown. Spoon off any excess fat and return all the pieces to the casserole. Add the vermouth or wine, increase the heat and cook until the liquid has almost evaporated.

4 Stir in the tomatoes, sugar, oregano, rosemary, bay leaf and 75 ml (2¼ fl oz) cold water. Bring everything to the boil, then stir in the reserved pancetta mixture. Cover, turn down the heat and leave to simmer for 30 minutes, or until the chicken is tender but not falling off the bone.

5 If the liquid is too thin, remove the chicken from the casserole, increase the heat and boil until the sauce has thickened. Discard the sprigs of herbs and taste for seasoning. Return the chicken to the casserole and add the additional oregano sprigs before serving.

MARINATED DUCK LEGS

SERVES 4

1 teaspoon juniper berries

2 garlic cloves, thickly sliced

4 x 20 cm (8 inch) rosemary sprigs, broken in half

125 ml (4 fl oz/½ cup) balsamic vinegar

4 large or 8 medium duck legs (about 875 g/1 lb 15 oz in total)

1 **To make the marinade,** squash the juniper berries with the back of a spoon to release their flavour. Put the berries in a shallow dish large enough to snugly fit the duck legs in one layer. Add the garlic, rosemary and balsamic vinegar, mixing everything together well.

2 **Trim the duck legs** of any excess fat. Put them, flesh side down, in the dish and leave to marinate for at least 1 hour or overnight in the fridge. Remove from the fridge about 15 minutes before roasting so they are not too cold.

3 **Preheat the oven** to 190°C (375°F/Gas 5). Remove the duck legs from the marinade and dry them on paper towels. Reserve the marinade.

4 **Heat an ovenproof frying pan** or casserole (one that will easily fit all the duck legs) over medium heat. Brown the legs, fat side first, so that the fat is released, creating enough oil to brown the skin. Once the duck is browned on both sides, arrange the legs neatly in one layer, cover and put the pan in the oven. The fat will slowly cook the flesh, keeping it moist while it cooks. Roast the duck for 1-1½ hours, or until the meat is very tender. Remove the lid for the last 30 minutes.

5 **Remove from the oven,** take out the legs and pour off any excess fat. Put the pan back on the stove, add the marinade, bring to the boil and cook for 5 minutes or until the sauce has reduced and thickened. If the sauce is too thick, dilute it with a dash of water. Put the duck legs back into the sauce. Allow the duck to rest for about 10 minutes before serving. Serve with gnocchi, polenta or lentils.

VINEGAR-POACHED CHICKEN

SERVES 4

4 x 500 g (1 lb 2 oz) small chickens or spatchcocks (poussin)

1 large carrot, chopped

1 large onion, chopped

1 celery stalk, chopped

bouquet garni

1½ tablespoons sugar

500 ml (16 fl oz/2 cups) white wine vinegar

3 tablespoons balsamic vinegar

1 tablespoon butter

1 tablespoon plain (all-purpose) flour

170 ml (6 fl oz/^{2}/3 cup) chicken stock

4 sprigs of rosemary

1 **Trim any fat** from the chickens and season well with salt and pepper, both inside and out. Tie the legs together and tuck the wings behind the chicken. Spread out the carrot, onion and celery in a casserole large enough to take the chickens side by side (don't add the chickens yet, though). Add the bouquet garni, sugar, white wine vinegar and balsamic vinegar and bring to the boil. Reduce the heat and simmer for 5 minutes.

2 **Place the chickens** on top of the vegetables, breast up. Add enough boiling water to cover the birds, put the lid on the casserole and simmer for 25 minutes, or until they are just cooked. Turn off the heat and leave the chickens in the casserole for 10 minutes.

3 **Melt the butter** in a small saucepan. Add the flour and cook, stirring, for 30 seconds. Gradually stir in the chicken stock and simmer until smooth and thickened. Stir in 3–4 tablespoons of the chicken poaching liquid and then taste. Continue adding a little poaching liquid (probably about 125 ml/½ cup in total) until the sauce is to your taste. Increase the heat and boil until slightly thickened. Season well with salt and pepper.

4 **Remove the chickens** from the casserole, drain well and arrange on a warm serving platter. Spoon just enough sauce over the chickens to glaze the skin, garnish with the rosemary sprigs and serve.

TURKEY SPIEDINI

SERVES 4

1 teaspoon fennel seeds
1 garlic clove
400 g (14 oz) minced (ground) turkey
2 tablespoons chopped oregano, marjoram or thyme
1 large lemon
1 thick slice of bread, crust removed, cut into 2 cm (¾ inch) cubes
8 bay leaves
1 tablespoon olive oil

1 **Put the fennel seeds** and garlic in a mortar and pestle and crush with a pinch of salt. If you don't have a mortar and pestle, crush them in a small bowl with the end of a rolling pin or in a spice grinder

2 **Mix the fennel and garlic** with the turkey mince and herbs and season with pepper. Test the seasoning by frying a teaspoon of the mixture in a little oil and tasting for flavour. peel the lemon completely, removing the zest and white pith. Cut the lemon into four thick slices, then cut the slices in half, making eight pieces (for a stronger flavour, use the lemon zest instead of the flesh). Roll the turkey into 16 small balls, pressing firmly so they won't break up when cooked.

3 **To assemble a kebab,** start with a piece of bread, spear it onto the skewer and push it to the end. Next, push on a ball of turkey and shape it to the thickness of the bread. Next, place a slice of lemon, followed by a turkey ball, a bay leaf, a piece of bread, a turkey ball, lemon slice, turkey ball, bay leaf and finish with a piece of bread. Put the kebabs on a plate and drizzle with olive oil (mostly over the bread so that it soaks up some of the oil).

4 **Heat a chargrill pan** or barbecue grill plate to very hot, then reduce the heat to medium.

5 **Season the kebabs** and cook for about 15 minutes, turning once. Check that the heat is not too high—the kebabs need to brown and cook through rather than burn on the outside. Squeeze a little lemon juice over the top before serving.

ROAST CHICKEN WITH ROSEMARY

SERVES 4

2 sprigs of rosemary

3 garlic cloves

1 teaspoon balsamic vinegar

1 x 1.5 kg (3 lb 5 oz) chicken

2 tablespoons extra virgin olive oil

2 tablespoons olive oil

125 ml (½ cup) chicken stock

1 Preheat the oven to 200°C (400°F/Gas 6). Put one rosemary sprig, the garlic and balsamic vinegar inside the cavity of the chicken. Add a large pinch of salt and a few grinds of black pepper. Truss the legs together.

2 Rub the extra virgin olive oil over the chicken skin. Pour the olive oil into a roasting tin and put the chicken in the tin, breast up. Place the second sprig of rosemary on top.

3 Transfer to the oven and roast for 1 hour, turning the chicken and basting with the pan juices every 15 minutes.

4 Put the chicken on a warm serving plate and discard the rosemary sprig. Spoon off the fat from the roasting tin and place it over high heat on the stovetop. Add the chicken stock and deglaze the pan. Boil until reduced and thickened. Taste for salt and pepper, then pour into a sauceboat to accompany the chicken. Serve with roast rosemary potatoes.

MEAT

PORK COOKED IN MILK

SERVES 4

2.25 kg (5 lb) pork loin, chined and skinned

50 ml (1¾ fl oz) olive oil

4 garlic cloves, cut in half lengthways

4 sage or rosemary sprigs

1 litre (35 fl oz/4 cups) milk

peeled zest of 2 lemons

juice of 1 lemon

1   Preheat the oven to 200°C (400°F/Gas 6). Heat the olive oil in a roasting tin. Add the pork and brown the meat on all sides. Remove the pork and pour away the fat in the roasting pan. Add the garlic and sage to the roasting tin and place the pork on top, bone side down. Season with salt and pepper and pour the milk over the pork. Return to the heat and bring just to the boil. Remove from the heat, add the lemon zest and drizzle with the lemon juice. The milk will start to curdle and might look alarming, but this is how the sauce is supposed to look.

2   Transfer the roasting tin to the oven and cook for about 20 minutes. Reduce the heat to 150°C (300°F/Gas 2) and cook for another 1–1¼ hours, depending on the thickness of the meat. If the milk evaporates before the end of cooking time, add a little more to keep the meat roasting in liquid. Baste the meat with the juices every 30 minutes. Do not cover, so that the juices reduce and the fat on the pork becomes crisp.

3   To test if the pork is cooked, poke a skewer into the middle of the meat, count to ten and pull it out. Touch it on the inside of your wrist: if it feels very hot, the meat is cooked through. Remove the pork from the oven and leave it to rest for at least 10 minutes. Remove the herbs and garlic.

4   Serve with wet polenta or roasted potatoes with a little of the sauce spooned over the top.

OSSO BUCO ALLA MILANESE

SERVES 4

12 pieces veal shank, about 4 cm
(1½ inch) thick

plain (all-purpose) flour, seasoned with
salt and pepper

3 tablespoons olive oil

60 g (2¼ oz) butter

1 garlic clove, finely chopped

1 onion, finely chopped

1 celery stalk, finely chopped

250 ml (9 fl oz/1 cup) dry white wine

1 bay leaf or lemon leaf

pinch of allspice

pinch of ground cinnamon

GREMOLATA

2 teaspoons grated lemon zest

2 tablespoons finely chopped flat-leaf
(Italian) parsley

1 garlic clove, finely chopped

1 **Dust each piece of veal shank** with seasoned flour. Heat the oil, butter, garlic, onion and celery in a heavy-based frying pan or saucepan that is big enough to hold the shanks in a single layer (but don't add the shanks yet). Cook for about 5 minutes over low heat until soft but not browned. Add the shanks to the pan and cook for 15 minutes, or until well browned all over. Arrange shanks in the pan, standing them up in a single layer. Add wine, bay leaf, allspice and cinnamon. Bring to the boil. Cover the pan. Turn the heat down to low.

2 **Cook at a low simmer** for 15 minutes, then add 125 ml (4 fl oz/½ cup) warm water. Continue cooking, covered, for about 45–60 minutes (the timing will depend on the age of the veal) or until the meat is tender and you can cut it with a fork. Check the volume of liquid once or twice during cooking time and add more warm water as needed.

3 **To make the gremolata,** mix together the lemon zest, parsley and garlic.

4 **Transfer the veal** shanks to a plate and keep warm. Discard the bay leaf. Increase the heat under the pan and stir for 1–2 minutes until the sauce has thickened, scraping up any bits off the bottom of the pan as you stir. Season with salt and pepper if necessary and return the veal shanks to the sauce. Heat everything through, then stir through half the gremolata. Serve sprinkled with the remaining gremolata. Usually accompanied by risotto alla milanese.

ROAST LAMB

SERVES 4

2 rosemary sprigs

3 garlic cloves

75 g (2½ oz) pancetta

2 kg (4 lb 8 oz) leg of lamb, shank bone cut off just above the joint, trimmed of excess fat and tied

1 large onion

125 ml (4 fl oz/½ cup) olive oil

375 ml (13 fl oz/1½ cups) dry white wine

1 **Preheat the oven** to 230°C (450°F/Gas 8). Strip the leaves off the rosemary sprigs and chop them with the garlic and pancetta until fine and paste-like (a food processor works well for this). Season with a little salt and plenty of pepper.

2 **With the point of a sharp knife,** make incisions about 1 cm (½ inch) deep all over the lamb. Rub the rosemary filling over the surface of the lamb, pushing it into the incisions.

3 **Cut the onion** into four thick slices and put them in the centre of a roasting tin. Place the lamb on top and gently pour the olive oil over it. Roast for 15 minutes. Reduce the temperature to 180°C (350°F/Gas 4) and pour in 250 ml (9 fl oz/1 cup) of the wine. Roast for 1½ hours for medium-rare, or longer if you prefer. Baste a couple of times and add a little water if the juices start to burn in the tin.

4 **Transfer the lamb** to a carving platter and leave to rest for 10 minutes. remove the onion (if it isn't burnt, serve it with the meat) and spoon off the excess fat from the tin. Place over high heat on the stovetop, pour in the remaining wine and cook for 3–4 minutes, or until the sauce reduces and slightly thickens. Taste for seasoning. Slice the lamb and serve with the sauce spooned over the top.

VEAL POLPETTE

SERVES 4

160 ml (5¼ fl oz) olive oil

1 onion, finely chopped

50 g (1¾ oz) pine nuts, roughly chopped

3 garlic cloves, finely chopped

40 g (1½ oz) parsley, roughly chopped, plus extra, to serve

15 g (½ oz) basil or rosemary, chopped

1 teaspoon fennel seeds, ground

50 g (1¾ oz) fresh breadcrumbs

200 g (7 oz) ricotta cheese

25 g (1 oz) parmesan cheese, grated

grated zest of 1 large lemon

500 g (1 lb 12 oz) minced veal

SAUCE

100 ml (3½ fl oz) red wine

800 g (1 lb 12 oz) tinned chopped tomatoes

1 Heat 3 tablespoons of the olive oil in a saucepan and cook the onion and pine nuts until the onion is soft. Add the garlic and cook for a few more minutes, then set aside to cool.

2 Put the herbs, fennel seeds, breadcrumbs, ricotta, parmesan and lemon zest in a bowl and add the mince. Add the cooled onion and pine nuts, season with salt and pepper and mix briefly until all ingredients are combined. Leave to rest in the fridge for at least 30 minutes or overnight.

3 For best results and to check for correct seasoning, cook one small meatball in a little of the oil while the rest of the mixture is resting in the fridge. Taste and adjust accordingly.

4 To make the polpette, roll the mixture into balls about the size of walnuts. Flatten them slightly to make it easier to cook them on both sides and push any pine nuts that are protruding back in or they will burn.

5 Heat the remaining oil in a large frying pan and cook the polpette over medium-high heat until golden brown. You might need to cook them in two batches but remove any sediment left in the pan after the first batch to prevent it burning. Make sure there is enough oil to prevent them from sticking to the pan. Remove the polpette and set aside.

6 For the sauce, drain all but 1 tablespoon of the olive oil from the pan, add the wine and cook for a few minutes to reduce the liquid. Add the tomatoes, season with salt and pepper and simmer for 15 minutes, breaking up any large chunks of tomato. Add the meatballs to the tomato sauce and reduce the heat to a gentle simmer.

7 Cover the pan and cook for a further 10 minutes, carefully turning the meatballs over in the sauce. Leave to rest for 10 minutes. Scatter with the extra parsley before serving.

BOLLITO MISTO WITH SALSA VERDE

SERVES 4

1 x 800 g (1 lb 12 oz) cotechino sausage

1 x 1.25 kg (2 lb 12 oz) small beef tongue

3 parsley sprigs

4 baby carrots

1 celery stalk, sliced

2 onions, roughly chopped

10 peppercorns

2 bay leaves

1 x 1.25 kg (2 lb 12 oz) beef brisket

1 large tomato or 1 tablespoon tomato purée

1 x 900 g (2 lb) chicken

12 whole baby turnips

18 small pickling or pearl onions

SALSA VERDE

1½ tablespoons fresh white breadcrumbs

1 tablespoon milk

1 hard-boiled egg yolk

2 anchovy fillets

1 tablespoon capers

5 tablespoons finely chopped parsley, mint and basil

1 garlic clove, crushed

75 ml (2¼ fl oz) extra virgin olive oil

1 **Put the sausage** in a pan of boiling water, reduce the heat, cover the pan and simmer for about 1½ hours, or until the sausage is tender. Leave in the cooking liquid until ready to use.

2 **Meanwhile,** bring a stockpot or very large saucepan of water to the boil. Add the tongue, parsley, carrots, celery, chopped onion, peppercorns, bay leaves and 1 teaspoon salt. Bring back to the boil, skim the surface and add the beef brisket and tomato. Cover, reduce the heat and simmer for 2 hours, skimming the surface from time to time.

3 **To make the salsa verde,** process or pound (in a mortar and pestle) everything together except the olive oil. Then whisk in the oil.

4 **Add the chicken,** turnips and onions to the stockpot and simmer for another hour. Top up with boiling water if necessary to keep the meat always covered. Add the cotechino for the last 20 minutes of cooking.

5 **Turn off the heat** and remove the tongue. Peel, trim and slice it, then arrange the slices on a warm platter. Slice the cotechino and beef and joint the chicken. Arrange all the meats on the platter and surround them with the carrots, turnips and onions. Moisten with a little of the cooking liquid, then take the platter to the table. Serve with the salsa verde and mostarda di Cremona.

VITELLO TONNATO

SERVES 4

1.25 kg (2 lb 12 oz) boneless rolled veal roast

500 ml (17 fl oz/2 cups) dry white wine

500 ml (17 fl oz/2 cups) chicken stock

2 garlic cloves

1 onion, quartered

1 carrot, roughly chopped

1 celery stalk, roughly chopped

2 bay leaves

3 cloves

10 peppercorns

SAUCE

95 g (3¼ oz) tinned tuna in olive oil, drained

15 g (½ oz) anchovy fillets

185 ml (6 fl oz/¾ cup) olive oil

2 egg yolks

2 tablespoons lemon juice

parsley sprigs, to serve

capers, rinsed and dried, to serve

thin lemon slices, to serve

1 Put the veal, wine, stock, garlic, onion, carrot, celery, bay leaves, cloves and peppercorns in a stockpot or very large saucepan. Add enough water to come two-thirds of the way up the veal and bring to the boil. Reduce the heat, cover the pan and simmer for 1¼ hours, or until tender.

2 Leave to cool for 30 minutes, then remove the veal from the pan and strain the stock. Pour the stock into a saucepan and boil rapidly until reduced to about 250 ml (9 fl oz/1 cup).

3 To make the sauce, purée the tuna with the anchovy fillets in a blender or small food processor with 3 tablespoons of the olive oil. Add the egg yolks and 1 tablespoon of the lemon juice and process until smooth. With the motor running, slowly pour in the rest of the oil. Gradually add the reduced stock until the sauce has the consistency of a thin mayonnaise. (If you are making the sauce by hand, chop the tuna and anchovy finely, mix in the egg yolks and lemon juice and then whisk in the stock.) Blend in the remaining lemon juice to taste, and season well. Chill until ready to serve.

4 To serve, thinly slice the cold veal and arrange in overlapping slices down the centre of a serving platter. Spoon the sauce over the top and garnish with the parsley, capers and lemon slices.

VENETIAN-STYLE LIVER

SERVES 4

800 g (1 lb 12 oz) calf's liver, very thinly
   sliced

2 tablespoons olive oil

60 g (2¼ oz) butter

2 large white onions, thinly sliced

1 tablespoon finely chopped flat-leaf
   (Italian) parsley

lemon wedges, to serve

1   **Trim the liver** of any straggly bits. Heat the olive oil and half the butter in a large frying pan and add the onion. Cover the pan and cook over low heat for 30–40 minutes, stirring from time to time, until the onion is very soft and golden. Season well with salt and pepper and transfer to a bowl.

2   **Melt the remaining butter** in the frying pan, increase the heat and fry the liver quickly to brown on both sides. Return the onion to the pan and cook, stirring often, for 1–2 minutes, or until the liver is browned on the outside but still a little pink in the middle—if you prefer your liver well cooked then keep going until it is brown all the way through.

3   **Remove from the heat**, stir in the parsley and check for seasoning. Serve with lemon wedges.

BISTECCA ALLA FIORENTINA

SERVES 4

2 x 1 kg (2 lb 4 oz) T-bone or sirloin
 steaks, about 3 cm (1¼ inch) thick

extra virgin olive oil

lemon wedges, to serve

1 Heat a griddle or barbecue grill plate and season the steak with salt and pepper. Brush the meat very lightly with olive oil to prevent too many flames appearing and cook at a fierce heat, turning once, to your taste (ideally rare or medium rare).

2 Test the steaks by pressing them and comparing this to the feeling of pressing the flesh at the base of your thumb. Rare meat will feel as your thumb feels when relaxed; for medium meat hold your thumb halfway across your palm; for well-done meat, hold your thumb all the way across your palm. This method is more accurate than timing as your heat source may be variable or your steak thinner or thicker.

3 Remove from the barbecue and serve on a large plate with a drizzle of good-quality extra virgin olive oil, some salt and pepper and a wedge of lemon.

4 A simple salad and potatoes, either roasted or fried, are perfect accompaniments, although usually the meat is too large to serve with anything else on the plate.

SAUSAGES COOKED WITH LENTILS

SERVES 4

3 tablespoons olive oil

8 Italian sausages

1 onion, chopped

3 garlic cloves, thinly sliced

2 tablespoons finely chopped rosemary

800 g (1 lb 12 oz) tinned tomatoes

16 juniper berries, lightly crushed

1 teaspoon freshly grated nutmeg

1 bay leaf

1 dried chilli

200 ml (7 fl oz) red wine

100 g (3½ oz) green lentils, such as Castelluccian or Puy lentils

1 Heat the olive oil in a large saucepan and cook the sausages for 5–10 minutes, browning well all over. Remove the sausages and set aside.

2 If the sausages burn the saucepan, wash it briefly before carrying on. If the pan is only slightly browned, this will enhance the flavour, so don't worry about cleaning it.

3 Reduce the heat to low, add the onion and garlic to the pan and cook until the onion is soft and translucent, but not browned. Stir in the rosemary, then add the tomatoes and cook gently until the sauce has thickened.

4 Add the juniper berries, nutmeg, bay leaf, chilli, red wine and 400 ml (14 fl oz) water. Bring to the boil, then add the lentils and the cooked sausages. Stir well, cover the saucepan and simmer gently for about 40 minutes, or until the lentils are soft. Stir the lentils a few times to prevent them sticking to the base of the pan and add a little more water if you need to cook them for a bit longer. Remove the bay leaf and chilli to serve.

SALTIMBOCCA

SERVES 4

8 small veal escalopes
8 slices prosciutto
8 sage leaves
2 tablespoons olive oil
60 g (2¼ oz) butter
185 ml (6 fl oz/¾ cup) dry Marsala or dry white wine

1   **Place the veal** between two sheets of greaseproof paper and pound with a meat mallet or rolling pin until they are 5 mm (¼ inch) thick. Make sure you pound them evenly. Peel off the paper and season lightly. Cut the prosciutto slices to the same size as the veal. Cover each piece of veal with a slice of prosciutto and place a sage leaf in the centre. Secure the sage leaf with a cocktail stick.

2   **Heat the olive oil** and half the butter in a large frying pan. Add the veal in batches and fry, prosciutto side up, over medium heat for 3–4 minutes, or until the veal is just cooked through. Briefly flip the saltimbocca over and fry the prosciutto side. Transfer each batch to a hot plate as it is done.

3   **Pour off the oil** from the pan and add the Marsala or wine. Bring to the boil and cook over high heat until reduced by half, scraping up the bits from the bottom of the pan. Add the remaining butter and, when it has melted, season the sauce. Remove the cocktail sticks and spoon the sauce over the veal to serve.

PORK CHOPS PIZZAIOLA

SERVES 4

4 pork chops

4 tablespoons olive oil

600 g (1 lb 5 oz) ripe tomatoes

3 garlic cloves, crushed

3 basil leaves, torn into pieces

1 teaspoon finely chopped parsley,
    to serve

1 **Using scissors** or a knife, cut the pork fat at 5 mm (¼ inch) intervals around the rind. Brush the chops with 1 tablespoon of the olive oil and season well.

2 **Remove the stems** from the tomatoes and score a cross in the bottom of each one. Blanch in boiling water for 30 seconds. Transfer to cold water, peel the skin away from the cross and chop the tomatoes.

3 **Heat** 2 tablespoons of the oil in a saucepan over low heat and add the garlic. Soften without browning for 1–2 minutes, then add the tomato and season. Increase the heat, bring to the boil and cook for 5 minutes until thick. Stir in the basil.

4 **Heat the remaining oil** in a large frying pan with a tight-fitting lid. Brown the chops in batches over medium-high heat for 2 minutes on each side. Place in a slightly overlapping row down the centre of the pan and spoon the sauce over the top, covering the chops completely. Cover the pan and cook over low heat for about 5 minutes. Sprinkle with parsley to serve.

RABBIT WITH FIGS AND SPICES

SERVES 4

4 tablespoons extra virgin olive oil

2 rabbits (900 g/2 lb total weight), each jointed into six portions

2 red onions, thinly sliced

1 large carrot, thinly sliced

3 large celery stalks, thinly sliced

2 garlic cloves, thinly sliced

2 rosemary sprigs, chopped

250 g (9 oz) dried figs, cut in half

2 small cinnamon sticks

12 juniper berries

200 ml (7 fl oz) white wine

1 litre (35 fl oz/4 cups) chicken stock

3 teaspoons cornflour (cornstarch)

1 dried red chilli

1   Heat the olive oil in a casserole over medium heat. Add the rabbit pieces in batches, gently brown on both sides and season with salt and pepper. Remove the meat from the casserole as it is browned. Preheat the oven to 150°C (300°F/Gas 3).

2   Add the onion and carrot to the casserole and gently cook until the onion is soft, then add the celery, garlic and rosemary and cook for another few minutes. Add the figs, cinnamon, juniper berries and wine, bring to the boil and cook for a couple of minutes until the wine has reduced.

3   Mix 3 tablespoons cold stock (or water) with the cornflour and stir until smooth. Add to the casserole with the remaining stock and bring to the boil, stirring frequently, for a minute to cook the cornflour. The sauce needs to be thick enough to lightly coat the vegetables so, if necessary, add a little more cornflour mixed with cold water.

4   Add the rabbit pieces and chilli and bring to the boil. Cover and cook in the oven for about 1 hour, or until the rabbit is tender enough to cut with a fork. Leave to rest for about 15 minutes before serving.

VENISON AL FORNO WITH TOMATOES AND PORCINI

SERVES 4

20 g (¾ oz) dried porcini mushrooms

750 g (1 lb 10 oz) venison, cut into 3 cm (1¼ inch) cubes

4 tablespoons extra virgin olive oil

1 onion, finely chopped

1 large celery stalk, finely chopped

1 large carrot, finely chopped

2 garlic cloves, finely chopped

2 sage sprigs, chopped

400 g (14 oz) tinned tomatoes

100 ml (3½ fl oz) red wine

1 Put the porcini in a bowl, cover with 200 ml (7 fl oz) hot water and leave to soak for 15 minutes. Preheat the oven to 150°C (300°F/Gas 3).

2 Heat the olive oil in a casserole, add the venison in batches and brown on both sides, moving the meat around when you first add it so it doesn't stick to the base and burn. Remove the meat from the casserole as it is browned.

3 Add the onion, celery and carrot to the casserole to make a soffritto and reduce the heat a little. Add the garlic and cook the vegetables for about 10 minutes, or until slightly soft and transparent. Drain the mushrooms, reserving the soaking liquid, and add them to the casserole with the sage. Stir briefly, then add the tomatoes, breaking them up with a spoon.

4 Add the wine and mushroom soaking liquid and cook, stirring every now and then, for another 10 minutes. Return the venison to the casserole, season with salt and pepper and bring just to the boil.

5 Cover the casserole and cook in the oven for about 2 hours. After the first 30 minutes, check that the meat is cooking at a gentle simmer, not too fast or too slow. When the meat is tender, set it aside for at least an hour or refrigerate overnight to let the flavours develop, then reheat gently just before serving.

FRITTO MISTO

SERVES 4

350 g (12 oz) fresh calves' sweetbreads

350 g (12 oz) fresh calves' brains

2 tablespoons vinegar or half a lemon

1 bay leaf

BATTER

50 g (1¾) plain (all-purpose) flour

2 teaspoons olive oil

3 egg whites

oil, for deep-frying

2 tablespoons capers, rinsed and squeezed dry

16 sage leaves

lemon wedges, to serve

1   To prepare the sweetbreads and brains, place them in cold water and leave to soak for at least 6 hours or overnight, changing the water several times until the water is clear and free of any blood. Rub your hands over the brains and sweetbreads to release any pockets of blood.

2   Place the offal in a saucepan, cover with cold water and add the vinegar or lemon, the bay leaf and a pinch of salt. Simmer for 3 minutes, remove from the heat and drain. Rinse in cold water and remove any outer skin or membrane. Cut the sweetbreads and brains into small chunks about 4 cm (1½ inches) wide.

3   To prepare the batter, put the flour in a bowl and make a well in the centre. Pour in the olive oil and a pinch of salt. Mix together with a wooden spoon or whisk, incorporating the flour from the edges into the centre so that it forms a paste. Add 75–100 ml (2¼–3½ fl oz) warm water and mix well, beating out any lumps. The consistency should be like thick cream. Leave to rest for at least 10 minutes. Whisk the egg whites in a bowl with a pinch of salt until they form soft peaks and fold them gently into the batter.

4   To cook the offal, heat the oil in a deep-fat fryer or fill a deep frying pan one-third full and heat to about 180°C (350°F), or until a piece of bread turns golden brown when dropped in the oil. If the oil starts to smoke, it is too hot.

5   Dip the sweetbreads and brains into the batter, coating all sides, and fry in the hot oil until golden brown. Fry in batches. Remove and drain on paper towels.

6   Add the capers and sage to the oil and fry quickly until crisp. Remove with a slotted spoon and scatter over the offal. Season with salt and serve immediately with the lemon wedges.

SALADS & SIDES

PANZANELLA

SERVES 4

900 g (2 lb) ripe tomatoes, peeled and quartered

3 garlic cloves, crushed

30 g (1 oz) basil, torn, plus a few whole leaves for garnishing

50 ml (1¾ fl oz) red wine vinegar

300 ml (10½ fl oz) extra virgin olive oil

1 day-old 'country-style' loaf, such as ciabatta, crust removed, cut into 4 cm (½ inch) cubes

1 small cucumber, peeled, deseeded

2 red capsicums (peppers), peeled and cut into 2 cm (¾ inch) strips

2 yellow capsicums (peppers), peeled and cut into 2 cm (¾ inch) strips

50 g (1¾ oz) capers, rinsed and dried

100 g (3½ oz) black olives, pitted and halved

30 g (1 oz) anchovies, cut in half lengthways

1 **Hold each tomato quarter** over a large bowl and squeeze out the seeds and juice. Add the garlic, half the basil, the vinegar and 200 ml (7 fl oz) of the olive oil. Taste for seasoning.

2 **Add the bread** to the bowl along with the tomato quarters. Leave for at least 30 minutes. If the bread is quite hard, it may need more liquid; if so, add more olive oil and vinegar in the same proportions.

3 **Just before serving,** thinly slice the cucumber and add to the bowl. To serve, divide half the salad among six plates. Top with half the capsicum, then sprinkle with half the capers, half the olives and anchovies and the remaining basil. Put the last of the bread mixture on top and repeat with the remaining capsicum, capers, olives, anchovies. Garnish with basil leaves and drizzle with the remaining olive oil just before serving. The salad can be left for up to 2 hours. Serve at room temperature.

CAPONATA

SERVES 4

2 large eggplants (aubergines), cut into 3 cm (1¼ inch) cubes

3 large celery stalks, finely chopped

3 tablespoons extra virgin olive oil

1 large onion, finely chopped

50 g (1¾ oz) pine nuts

4 garlic cloves, thinly sliced

400 g (14 oz) tomatoes, peeled or 400 g (14 oz) tinned chopped tomatoes

olive oil, for shallow-frying

1 teaspoon dried oregano

3 tablespoons capers, rinsed and dried

4 tablespoons red wine vinegar

12 green olives, pitted and chopped

1 **Put the eggplant** in layers in a colander, sprinkling salt on each layer. Leave the aubergines to degorge (give off any bitter juices) for about 20 minutes, then rinse in cold water and squeeze dry with your hands.

2 **Put the eggplant** in a large bowl.

3 **Blanch the celery** in boiling water for 1 minute then plunge into cold water, drain and set aside. (Blanching dilutes the flavour of the celery a little as it can be quite overpowering.)

4 **Heat the extra virgin olive oil** in a saucepan over low heat and cook the onion and pine nuts until the onion is soft and the pine nuts are light brown. Add the garlic and cook for another minute. Add the celery and tomatoes and cook until the sauce has thickened.

5 **Pour a generous amount of olive oil** into a deep frying pan. To test the oil is deep enough, hold a teaspoon upright in the pan: the oil should reach a quarter of the way up the spoon. Add enough eggplant to just cover the base of the pan and cook over medium heat until golden brown and soft on both sides. Remove from the pan and place in a colander to drain off any oil. Repeat until all the eggplant is cooked.

6 **Add the oregano,** capers and red wine vinegar to the tomato sauce. Bring to the boil and simmer gently until thickened. Remove from the heat and add the eggplant and olives. Stir briefly and season with salt and pepper. Leave to rest for at least 15 minutes before serving.

INSALATA CAPRESE

SERVES 4

8 ripe plum tomatoes

3–4 mozzarella balls

2 tablespoons extra virgin olive oil

15 small basil leaves

1 Slice the tomatoes, pouring off any excess juice, and cut the mozzarella into slices of a similar thickness.

2 Arrange alternating rows of tomato and mozzarella on a serving plate. Sprinkle with salt and pepper and drizzle the olive oil over the top. Scatter with basil leaves, tearing any large ones. Serve immediately.

TRUFFLE AND ROCKET SALAD

BRUSCHETTA

6 slices sourdough bread

1 garlic clove

2 tablespoons extra virgin olive oil

180 g (6 oz) rocket (arugula)

1 tablespoon lemon juice

3–4 tablespoons extra virgin olive oil, plus extra for drizzling

1 small truffle

parmesan cheese, to serve

1 To make the bruschetta, grill (broil), chargrill or toast the bread until it is crisp. Cut the garlic clove in half and rub the cut edge over both sides of the bread, then drizzle a little olive oil over each slice.

2 Put the rocket in a bowl and dress with the lemon juice, olive oil, salt and pepper. Mix together gently and divide among six plates.

3 Thinly slice the truffle, ideally using a truffle slicer or sharp mandolin. Slice the truffle over each plate—the pieces should be as thin as possible and will break up easily if touched by hand. Shave slivers of parmesan off the block with a potato peeler, mandolin or sharp knife.

4 Arrange the parmesan around the truffle (you won't need much parmesan: you don't want to overwhelm the truffle) and drizzle with a little olive oil. Serve with the pieces of bruschetta.

INSALATA DI RINFORZO

SERVES 4

50 g (1¾ oz) carrots

150 g (5½ oz) green beans

½ red onion

600 ml (21 fl oz) white wine vinegar

1 tablespoon sea salt

1 tablespoon sugar

1 bay leaf

300 g (10½ oz) cauliflower florets

DRESSING

4 tablespoons extra virgin olive oil

2 tablespoons lemon juice

1 tablespoon finely chopped parsley

1 tablespoon chopped capers

1 garlic clove, halved

4 anchovy fillets, halved lengthways

85 g (3 oz) small black olives, such as
  Gaeta or Ligurian

1 tablespoon roughly chopped flat-leaf
  (Italian) parsley

½ tablespoon extra virgin olive oil

1 **Cut the carrots** into batons about the size of your little finger. Cut the beans into similar lengths and slice the onion thinly.put the vinegar, sea salt, sugar and bay leaf in a saucepan with 500 ml (17 fl oz/2 cups) water and bring to the boil. Cook the carrots for about 3 minutes, or until crisp but tender, and transfer to a bowl with a slotted spoon. Add the beans to the pan and cook for 2 minutes, then add them to the bowl. Add the onion and cauliflower to the pan and cook for 3 minutes, or until the cauliflower just starts to soften. Drain, add to the bowl and allow the vegetables to cool.

2 **To make the dressing,** mix together the olive oil, lemon juice, parsley, capers and garlic and season well. Pour over the cooled vegetables and toss gently.

3 **To serve,** toss the anchovy fillets, olives, parsley and oil through the salad.

BORLOTTI BEANS WITH TOMATOES

SERVES 4

250 g (9 oz) fresh borlotti beans,
    200 g (7 oz) dried beans or 800 g
    (1 lb 12 oz) tinned beans

3 garlic cloves, unpeeled

1 bay leaf

4 tablespoons extra virgin olive oil

3 tablespoons red wine vinegar or
    balsamic vinegar

2 tomatoes, peeled and finely chopped

½ large mild red chilli, finely chopped

3 tablespoons roughly chopped mint

3 tablespoons roughly chopped parsley

1 If using fresh beans, there is no need to soak and precook them. If using dried beans, soak them in cold water for at least 6 hours or overnight. Drain the beans, put them in a saucepan, cover with water and bring to the boil. Drain again, rinsing away any foam that has appeared on the surface of the water. If using tinned beans, simply rinse well and drain before mixing with the olive oil and vinegar below.

2 To cook the fresh or dried beans, cover with water and bring to the boil, add the garlic, bay leaf and 1 tablespoon of the olive oil. Reduce the heat and simmer gently for about 20–30 minutes for fresh beans and about 40 minutes for dried, or until tender. Do not salt the beans during cooking as this will toughen the skins. Drain the beans, keeping the garlic.

3 Remove the skin from the garlic and mash with a fork (they will be quite soft after cooking and will easily break up). While the beans are still hot, mix in the rest of the oil, the vinegar and salt and pepper. Stir in the tomato, chilli and herbs just before serving.

GRILLED VEGETABLE SALAD

SERVES 4

1 yellow capsicum (pepper), grilled and peeled

1 red capsicum (pepper), grilled and peeled

2 eggplants (aubergines), sliced diagonally

4 zucchini (courgettes), sliced diagonally

DRESSING

2 garlic cloves

1 heaped teaspoon sea salt

150 ml (5 fl oz) extra virgin olive oil

juice of 1 small lemon or

3 tablespoons red wine vinegar

½ red chilli, finely chopped

15 g (¼ oz) basil, torn

6 peppercorns, crushed

1 Cut the yellow and red capsicums into wide strips and set aside.

2 Preheat a chargrill pan or barbecue grill plate to very hot. Place a few eggplant slices on the griddle and cook over medium-high heat, turning once, until the eggplant are soft and cooked. Cook all the eggplant in this way, stacking them up on top of each other once they're cooked, to help them steam a little and soften. Cook the zucchini slices in the same way until dark golden brown and add to the eggplant.

3 To make the dressing, smash the garlic cloves with the sea salt in a mortar and pestle. Alternatively, crush the garlic with a little salt using the flat blade of your knife. To do this, coat the knife blade in the salt and scrape it against the garlic in a downwards motion until it forms a paste. Mix together the garlic, olive oil, lemon juice, chilli, basil and peppercorns.

4 Place all the vegetables in a flat dish and pour over the dressing. Mix briefly to avoid breaking up the eggplant and leave to marinate for at least 30 minutes.

Note: The vegetables can be prepared a day in advance and left to marinate in the dressing overnight but mix in the basil just before serving.

BRAISED FENNEL WITH OLIVES

SERVES 4

2 large fennel bulbs

4 tablespoons extra virgin olive oil

1 red onion, halved and thinly sliced

3 garlic cloves, sliced

4 small sprigs of rosemary, chopped

100 ml (3½ fl oz) white wine

50 g (1¾ oz) black olives, pitted and halved

1 Slice the fennel into thick wedges, cutting from top to bottom but keeping them joined at the root. Cut off and reserve any fronds. Heat the olive oil in a large frying pan and cook the fennel and onion over medium heat for about 10 minutes, stirring occasionally until lightly browned.

2 Add the garlic and half the rosemary, season with salt and pepper and stir briefly to prevent the fennel and garlic from burning. After a few minutes, add the wine, put the lid on and gently cook for another 10–15 minutes, or until tender but still holding together. Lift the lid occasionally to make sure the fennel is not burning.

3 Once the fennel is soft it is cooked. If all the liquid has evaporated and the fennel is still not cooked, add a little more wine or water. Alternatively, if there is still a lot of liquid left and the fennel is almost cooked, lift the lid to allow the liquid to reduce a little. The fennel should be moist but not dry.

4 Add the olives and the rest of the chopped rosemary just before the end of cooking time. Serve sprinkled with any reserved fennel fronds.

OVEN-ROASTED TOMATOES

SERVES 4

12 large ripe tomatoes

150 ml (5 fl oz) extra virgin olive oil

3 garlic cloves, chopped

2 tablespoons finely chopped thyme
or rosemary

6 tablespoons finely chopped parsley

1   Slice the tomatoes in half horizontally. Put them on a lightly greased baking tray or in a very shallow gratin dish and season with salt and pepper. Preheat the oven to 175°C (350°F/Gas 4).

2   Combine the oil, garlic, thyme and parsley. Drizzle 2 teaspoons over the top of each tomato, then bake for 2–3 hours. The tomatoes should be caramelised and crisp on top and quite shrivelled, with all the liquid having reduced inside them. If the tomatoes are cooking too quickly and are starting to overbrown or burn, turn the heat down. If there is a lot of oil (the oil collects around the tomatoes), baste the tomatoes as they cook to keep the tops moist.

CHICORY, RADICCHIO AND PANCETTA AL FORNO

SERVES 4

450 g (1 lb) white chicory
1 large radicchio
150 g (5½ oz) pancetta or smoked bacon, thinly sliced
50 g (1¾ oz) fresh breadcrumbs
50 g (1¾ oz) parmesan cheese, grated
1½ tablespoons finely chopped thyme
1 garlic clove, finely chopped
570 ml (20 fl oz) thick (double/heavy) cream

1 **Preheat the oven** to 180°C (350°F/Gas 4). Slice the chicory in half lengthways (or if they are quite large, slice them into quarters). Divide the radicchio into six or eight wedges, depending on its size.

2 **Lightly butter a shallow** 2.5 litre (85 fl oz/10 cups) gratin dish. Place the chicory and radicchio in the dish in one layer, alternating the colours.

3 **Mix together** the pancetta, breadcrumbs, parmesan, thyme and garlic and season well. Sprinkle over the chicory and radicchio.

4 **Pour the cream** over the top, cover with foil and bake for 50–60 minutes. Take the foil off the dish for the last 20 minutes to crisp up the pancetta and breadcrumbs. Leave to rest for about 10 minutes before serving.

CANNELLINI BEAN AND GREMOLATA SALAD

SERVES 4

350 g (12 oz) dried cannellini or flageolet beans

3 garlic cloves, unpeeled

1 bay leaf

2 tablespoons extra virgin olive oil

3 red or yellow capsicums (peppers), peeled and cut into strips

drizzle of extra virgin olive oil and 1 tablespoon chopped parsley, to serve

DRESSING

4 tablespoons extra virgin olive oil

juice of 1 large lemon

GREMOLATA

2 garlic cloves

1 heaped teaspoon sea salt

grated zest of 1 large lemon

4 tablespoons chopped flat-leaf (Italian) parsley

1 **Soak the beans** in cold water for at least 6 hours. Drain the beans, put them in a saucepan, cover with water and bring to the boil. Drain again, rinsing away any foam that has appeared on the surface of the water.

2 **Cover the beans** with water again and bring to the boil. Add the garlic, bay leaf and olive oil. Simmer gently for about 40 minutes, or until tender (older drier beans will take longer to soften). Do not salt the beans during cooking as this will toughen the skins.

3 **Meanwhile,** make a dressing with the olive oil, lemon juice and salt and pepper. Drain the beans, remove the garlic and, while still hot, pour the dressing over the top and mix together.

4 **To make a gremolata,** smash the garlic cloves with the sea salt in a mortar and pestle. Alternatively, crush the garlic with a little salt using the flat blade of your knife. To do this, coat the knife blade in the salt and scrape it against the garlic in a downwards motion until it forms a paste. Using a fork, mix the garlic with the lemon zest, parsley and salt and pepper.

5 **Just before serving,** stir the gremolata through the beans. Spread the peppers over the beans and serve sprinkled with a little parsley and a drizzle of olive oil.

ARTICHOKE FRITTATA

SERVES 4

175 g (6 oz) broad beans, fresh or frozen
400 g (14 oz) tinned artichoke hearts, drained
3 tablespoons olive oil
1 onion, thinly sliced
6 eggs
2 tablespoons chopped parsley
45 g (1½ oz) pecorino cheese, grated
pinch of nutmeg

1 **Bring a small saucepan** of water to the boil and add a large pinch of salt and the broad beans. Boil for 2 minutes, then drain and rinse under cold water. Peel off the skins from the beans. cut the artichoke hearts from bottom to top into slices about 5 mm (¼ inch) wide. Discard any slices that contain the tough central choke.

2 **Heat the oil** in a 30 cm (12 inch) frying pan and fry the onion over low heat for 6–8 minutes, without allowing it to brown. Add the artichoke slices and cook for 1–2 minutes. Stir in the broad beans.

3 **Preheat the grill (broiler).** Lightly beat together the eggs, parsley, pecorino and nutmeg and season well. Pour into the frying pan and cook over low heat until three-quarters set, shaking the pan often to stop the frittata sticking.

4 **Finish the top** off under the grill and leave to cool before serving in wedges.

BRAISED ARTICHOKES WITH PEAS AND BROAD BEANS

SERVES 4

750 g (1 lb 10 oz) cleaned artichoke
hearts

1 kg (2 lb 4 oz) fresh broad beans in
pods (300 g/10½ oz) podded weight)

400 g (14 oz) fresh peas in pods
(150 g/5½ oz podded weight)

3 tablespoons extra virgin olive oil

1 red onion, quartered and thinly sliced

185 g (6½ oz) smoked pancetta

2 garlic cloves, chopped

125 ml (4 fl oz/½ cup) white wine

2 tablespoons chopped mint

1 Cut each artichoke heart into 12 segments. Pod the broad beans and peas and blanch them for 1 minute in boiling water, then refresh in iced water.

2 If the broad beans are very large and old you may also want to remove the pale green outer skin which can be very leathery.

3 Heat the olive oil in a large saucepan or deep frying pan and add the artichoke, onion and pancetta. Cook gently for about 15 minutes, stirring frequently. Season with salt and pepper. Add the broad beans and peas and cook for 5 minutes. (If the broad beans are large, add them before the peas as they will need a minute or two longer.) Stir in the garlic, add the wine and cook for 10 minutes more, or until all the liquid has evaporated.

4 Pierce the artichokes with a knife to see if they are tender. If they need more cooking, add a dash of water and cover. When cooked, add the mint, taste for seasoning and leave to stand for a few minutes to allow the flavours to develop.

Note: This dish is delicious served with grilled fish.

EGGPLANT PARMIGIANA

SERVES 4

1.5 kg (3 lb 5 oz) eggplants (aubergines)
plain (all-purpose) flour, seasoned with salt and pepper
350 ml (12 fl oz) olive oil
500 ml (17 fl oz/2 cups) tomato passata or tomato pasta sauce
2 tablespoons roughly torn basil leaves
250 g (9 oz) mozzarella, chopped
90 g (3¼ oz) parmesan cheese, grated

1   Thinly slice the eggplants lengthways. Layer the slices in a large colander, sprinkling salt between each layer. Leave for 1 hour to degorge. Rinse and pat the slices dry on both sides with paper towels, then coat lightly with the flour.

2   Preheat the oven to 180°C (350°F/Gas 4) and grease a shallow 2.5 litre (85 fl oz/10 cups) baking dish.

3   Heat 125 ml (4 fl oz/½ cup) of the olive oil in a large frying pan. Quickly fry the eggplant slices in batches over high heat until crisp and golden on both sides. Add more olive oil as needed and drain on paper towels as you remove each batch from the pan.

4   Make a slightly overlapping layer of eggplant slices over the base of the dish. Season with pepper and a little salt. Spoon 4 tablespoons of passata over the eggplant and scatter some of the basil over the top. Sprinkle with some mozzarella, followed by some parmesan. Continue with this layering until you have used up all the ingredients, then finish with a layer of the cheeses.

5   Bake for 30 minutes. Remove from the oven and allow to cool for 30 minutes before serving.

POTATO AND TOMATO AL FORNO

SERVES 4

120 ml (4 fl oz) extra virgin olive oil

1 large red onion, halved and thinly sliced

3 garlic cloves, sliced

500 g (1 lb 2 oz) ripe tomatoes, peeled and cut into large cubes

1 kg (2 lb 4 oz) waxy potatoes, unpeeled, cut into thick slices or wedges

15 g (¼ oz) rosemary or oregano, roughly chopped

16 black olives, pitted and chopped

4 tablespoons red wine vinegar

1 Preheat the oven to 200°C (400°F/Gas 6). Heat half the olive oil in a pan and cook the onion and garlic until the onion is soft and translucent.

2 Combine the tomatoes, onion, potatoes, herbs, olives, vinegar and the remaining olive oil and season well.

3 Spoon into a shallow 2.5 litre (85 fl oz/10 cups) gratin dish and bake for 1–1½ hours, until the tomato juices and dressing have been absorbed by the potatoes and they are soft and golden on top. If the tops of the potatoes start to overbrown, cover them loosely with a piece of foil until they are cooked through—they should be tender to the point of a knife.

POTATO AND LEEK AL FORNO

SERVES 4

1 kg (2 lb 4 oz) waxy potatoes, unpeeled
3 tablespoons butter or olive oil
400 g (14 oz) leeks, trimmed, halved and sliced
3 garlic cloves, thinly sliced
1 tablespoon chopped thyme or rosemary
300 g (10½ oz) mascarpone
250 ml (9 fl oz/1 cup) white wine

1 **Thinly slice the potatoes** with a mandolin or very sharp knife (they have to be the same thickness or they will not cook through evenly). Preheat the oven to 180°C (350°F/Gas 4). Heat the butter or oil in a saucepan and cook the leeks over low heat for about 10 minutes, or until soft. Season with salt and pepper. Add the garlic and herbs and cook for a couple of minutes.

2 **Grease a shallow** 3 litre (102 fl oz/12 cups) gratin dish with butter or oil. Arrange a layer of potatoes in the base of the dish and season with salt and pepper. Scatter with one-third of the leeks and a few dollops of mascarpone. Continue in the same way to make two more layers, finishing with a layer of potatoes (but not leeks as they will burn) and top with mascarpone. Pour the wine over the top and cover with foil.

3 **Bake in the oven** for about 1 hour, removing the foil for the last 15 minutes to brown and crisp the top.

VEGETABLE TORTE

SERVES 4

150 g (5½ oz) asparagus

4 tablespoons olive oil

1 onion, chopped

1 zucchini (courgette), halved lengthways and finely sliced

2 garlic cloves, chopped

100 g (3½ oz) spinach, stalks removed if necessary, roughly chopped

2 tablespoons chopped basil

75 g (2½ oz) parmesan cheese, grated

250 g (9 oz) ricotta cheese

250 g (9 oz) mascarpone

6 eggs

1 **Wash the asparagus** and remove the woody ends (hold each spear at both ends and bend it gently—it will snap at its natural breaking point). Remove the spear tips of the asparagus and slice the remaining stems. Bring a small saucepan of salted water to the boil and cook the asparagus stems for about 2 minutes. Add the tips and cook for 1 minute. Drain the asparagus and set aside.

2 **Preheat the oven** to 180°C (350°F/Gas 4). Heat the olive oil in a saucepan and cook the onion until soft. Increase the heat and add the zucchini. Cook until the zucchini is soft and a little golden brown, stirring occasionally. Add the garlic and cook for 1 minute more. Add the spinach and mix briefly until just wilted and cooked.

3 **Remove the pan from the heat,** add the asparagus and basil, season with salt and pepper and set aside to cool.

4 **Grease** a 20 cm (8 inch) spring-form cake tin with butter and dust with a tablespoon of the parmesan. Mix the ricotta, mascarpone, eggs and 50 g (1¾ oz) parmesan into the cooled vegetables and taste for seasoning.

5 **Spoon into the tin** and scatter with the remaining parmesan. Place the tin on a tray (to catch any drips) and bake for 50–60 minutes. The top should be a light golden brown and the mixture should still wobble slightly in the centre. Cool for 30 minutes, then chill in the fridge for 3 hours, or until the torte has set.

SERVES 4

MARINATED ZUCCHINI

500 g (1 lb 2 oz) small zucchini (courgettes)

1 tablespoon olive oil

1 tablespoon finely chopped parsley

1 garlic clove, sliced

1 tablespoon balsamic or red wine vinegar

SAUTÉED SPINACH

1 kg (2 lb 4 oz) spinach

2 tablespoons olive oil

1 garlic clove

GREEN BEANS

500 g (1 lb 2 oz) green beans, topped and tailed

1 tablespoon olive oil

MASHED POTATO

900 g (2 1b) mealy potatoes

185 ml (6 fl oz/¾ cup) milk

70 g (2½ oz) parmesan cheese, grated

freshly ground nutmeg

1 Thinly slice the zucchini diagonally. Heat the oil in a heavy-based frying pan and fry the slices on both sides until browned. Remove with a slotted spoon and drain. Put the zucchini in a non-metallic dish and add the remaining ingredients. Season well and leave for a few hours. Serve with grilled or roast meats or as an antipasto.

2 Wash the spinach thoroughly and shake it dry, leaving just a little water clinging to the leaves. Heat the oil in a frying pan and add the garlic. Cook for a few seconds and then add the spinach. Cover the pan for a minute to create some steam. Remove the lid and turn up the heat, stirring the spinach until all the liquid has evaporated. Season before serving.

3 Cook the beans in boiling salted water for 5 minutes, then drain and refresh. Drain thoroughly. Heat the oil in a frying pan and add the beans. Toss them in the oil for a minute or two and then season well.

4 Cut the potatoes into large even pieces and cook them in boiling salted water for about 12 minutes, or until they are tender to the point of a knife. Drain well. Put the milk in the saucepan and heat it briefly, then add the potatoes and mash until very smooth. Beat in the olive oil and parmesan and season with salt, pepper and nutmeg.

BREAD & PIZZA

BREAD DOUGH

MAKES 1

185 ml (6 fl oz/¾ cup) lukewarm milk

2 teaspoons honey

3 tablespoons warm water.

7 g (¼ oz) fresh yeast or 1 teaspoon
 dried yeast

125 g (4½ oz) plain (all-purpose) flour

7 g (¼ oz) fresh yeast or 1 teaspoon
 dried yeast

2½ teaspoons salt

500 g (1 lb 2 oz) plain (all-purpose) flour

1   To make the starter, mix the milk and honey in a large bowl with 3 tablespoons warm water. Sprinkle fresh or dried yeast over the top and stir to dissolve. Leave in a draught-free spot to activate. If the yeast does not bubble and foam in 5 minutes it is dead, so throw it away and start again. Add plain flour and whisk to form a thick paste. Cover loosely with clingfilm and leave overnight at room temperature to develop.

2   To make the dough, sprinkle the fresh or dried yeast over the starter. Break up the starter by squeezing it between your fingertips. Gradually add 250 ml (9 fl oz/1 cup) water, combining it with the starter. Mix in salt and plain flour with your fingers until the mixture comes together to form a soft dough. Turn out the dough onto a lightly floured work surface and knead for 10 minutes or until it is smooth and elastic and a finger indent pops

3   Place the dough in a lightly oiled bowl and cover with a damp dish towel. Allow to rise in a draft-free place for 1-1½ hours or until doubled in size. Knock back the dough by punching your fist into the middle of it. This deflates the air bubbles. Turn out the dough onto a lightly floured surface and knead for 1-2 minutes until it is very smooth and all the air bubbles have been knocked out. The dough is now ready to use.

Note: It is very important to knead bread dough properly. This generally means that it will take longer than you anticipated—sometimes up to 10 or 15 minutes. The more you knead the dough, the better the outcome will be. You can use the dough hook on a food mixer if you like.

MAKES 4–6

2 teaspoons flour

7 g (¼ oz) fresh yeast or 1 teaspoon dried yeast

600 g (1 lb 5 oz) plain (all-purpose) flour

2 teaspoons sea salt,

1 tablespoon olive oil

1 Mix flour in a large bowl with 3 tablespoons lukewarm water. Sprinkle fresh or dried yeast over the top and stir to dissolve. Leave in a draught-free spot to activate. If the yeast does not bubble and foam in 5 minutes it is dead, so throw it away and start again. Put plain flour, the yeast, sea salt, 300 ml (10½ fl oz) water and olive oil in a large bowl or in a food mixer with a dough hook.

2 Mix to form a dough, turn out onto a floured surface and knead for about 5 minutes. For pizzas, the dough does not have to be kneaded as well as it does for bread as it will be rolled out thinly and doesn't need to rise. Put the dough back in the bowl and smear with a film of oil to prevent it drying out. Cover and leave in a draught-free spot for about 2 hours or until doubled in size. Knock back the dough by punching your fist into the middle of it. Turn the dough out onto a lightly floured work surface and divide into four or six portions.

3 Dust with a little flour and roll into small balls. Try to make the surface as smooth as possible so that when the dough is rolled out it will not bubble too much. Put the balls on a tray or board dusted with a little flour and cover. Leave to rest for between 30 minutes and 2 hours. Heavily dust the work surface with flour to prevent the dough sticking, then flatten each ball into a circle. Finish off with a rolling pin to make a thin crust about 5 mm (¼ inch) thick, leaving a small ridge around the edge to hold the filling.

Note: Bear in mind that bread dough rises in the oven. This means that if you want a pizza with a thin crust you will need to roll the base very thinly. Leave a small ridge around the edge to stop the filling running out.

FOCACCIA

SERVES 4

15 g (¼ oz) fresh yeast or 2 teaspoons
    dried yeast

1 teaspoon sugar

400 g (14 oz) strong white flour

100 ml (3½ fl oz) extra virgin olive oil

large pinch of salt

20–24 small rosemary sprigs

coarse sea salt

1 Put the yeast in a bowl with the sugar and stir in 250 ml (9 fl oz/1 cup) lukewarm water. Leave in a draught-free spot to activate. If the yeast does not bubble and foam in 5 minutes it is dead, so throw it away and start again.

2 Put the flour, 50 ml (1¾ fl oz) of the olive oil and the salt in a large bowl or in a food mixer with a dough hook attachment and pour the yeast mixture into the middle. Knead the dough for about 5 minutes, either using the dough hook or with your hands on the work surface, until it forms a soft and slightly sticky ball.

3 Put the dough in a lightly greased bowl and smear with a film of oil to prevent it drying out. Cover with a tea towel (dish towel) and leave to rise in a warm place for about 2 hours or until doubled in size.

4 Knock back the dough to its original size by punching it with your fist. Press the dough into a greased 20 x 30 cm (8 x 12 inch) baking tray. Cover with a damp cloth and leave to rise for 30 minutes.

5 Preheat the oven to 220°C (425°F/Gas 7). Press deep dimples all over the surface of the dough with your fingertips. Put a rosemary sprig in each dimple. Bake for 20 minutes, or until golden brown. As soon as the focaccia comes out of the oven, drizzle it with the remaining oil and sprinkle with coarse salt. Serve warm.

GRISSINI

SERVES 4

1 tablespoon malt syrup

15 g (¼ oz) fresh yeast or 2 teaspoons dried yeast

500 g (1 lb 2 oz) plain (all-purpose) flour

1½ teaspoons salt

2 tablespoons olive oil

fine semolina, for dusting

1 **Put** 310 ml (10¾ fl oz/1¼ cups) warm water in a bowl and stir in the malt and yeast. Leave in a draught-free spot to activate. If the yeast does not bubble and foam in 5 minutes it is dead, so throw it away and start again. Sift the flour and salt into another bowl, add the yeast and the oil and mix until the dough clumps together.

2 **Form into a ball** and knead on a lightly floured surface for 5–6 minutes, or until the dough is smooth and elastic. Put the dough on a lightly oiled tray and squash out to fill the shape of the tray. Brush with oil to stop it sticking and slide the tray into a plastic bag. Leave for 1 hour until doubled in size.

3 **Preheat** the oven to 230°C (450°F/Gas 8) and lightly oil two baking trays. Sprinkle the dough with semolina. Cut the dough into four portions along its length, then slice each one into five strips. Pick up each strip by both ends and stretch out to at least 20 cm (8 inches) long, Try to keep the grissini as evenly shaped as you can so that they cook at the same rate.

4 **Arrange the grissini** on the trays, spacing them out a little. Dust lightly with flour. Bake for 20 minutes, or until crisp and golden. Cool slightly on the trays and then on wire racks.

PIZZA MARGHERITA

MAKES 1 X 30 CM (12 INCH) PIZZA

120 g (4¼ oz) ripe plum tomatoes

3 basil leaves

2 garlic cloves, crushed

1 tablespoon tomato passata

2 teaspoons extra virgin olive oil

1 x 30 cm (12 inch) pizza base (see page 125)

3 tablespoons extra virgin olive oil

150 g (5½ oz) mozzarella, chopped

9 small basil leaves

1 Core the tomatoes and purée in a food processor with the basil leaves (or chop the tomatoes and basil very finely and stir together). Stir in the garlic, passata and olive oil and season well. Leave for at least 30 minutes to allow the flavours to blend.

2 Preheat the oven to very hot and put a baking tray or pizza stone in the oven to heat up. Drizzle the pizza base with 2 tablespoons of the oil and spread with the tomato sauce. Scatter with the mozzarella and drizzle with the remaining olive oil. Slide onto the hot tray or stone (if you're not confident doing this, you can construct and bake the pizza on a cold tray, but the base won't be as crisp).

3 Cook for 2–12 minutes (this will depend on how hot your oven is), or until the base is light brown and crisp and the topping is cooked. Before serving, drizzle with a little more oil and scatter the basil over the top.

POTATO AND ROCKET PIZZA

MAKES 1 X 30 CM (12 INCH) PIZZA

1 x 30 cm (12 inch) pizza base (see page 125)

2 tablespoons extra virgin olive oil

1 potato, very thinly sliced

100 g (3½ oz) taleggio cheese, cut into small pieces

10 g (¼ oz) rocket (arugula)

extra virgin olive oil, for drizzling

1 **Preheat the oven** to very hot and put a baking tray or pizza stone in the oven to heat up. Drizzle the pizza base with oil. Cover with a layer of potato, leaving a thin border, sprinkle with the taleggio and season. Slide onto the hot tray or stone (if you're not confident doing this, you can construct and bake the pizza on a cold tray, but the base won't be as crisp).

2 **Cook** for 2–12 minutes (this will depend on how hot your oven is), or until the potato is cooked. Drizzle with oil and scatter with rocket.

WILD MUSHROOM PIZZA

MAKES 1 X 30 CM (12 INCH) PIZZA

100 g (3½ oz) fresh wild mushrooms,
  such as chanterelles or porcini,
  trimmed but left whole

3 tablespoons extra virgin olive oil

1 x 30 cm (12 inch) pizza base (see
  page 125)

1 tablespoon chopped thyme

2 small garlic cloves, chopped

extra virgin olive oil, for drizzling

1 **Preheat the oven** to very hot and put a baking tray or pizza stone in the oven to heat up. Toss the mushrooms in a tablespoon of the oil.

2 **Drizzle the pizza base** with oil and scatter with thyme and garlic. Top with the mushrooms and season. Slide onto the hot tray or stone (if you're not confident doing this, you can construct and bake the pizza on a cold tray, but it won't be as crisp).

3 **Cook** for 2–12 minutes (this will depend on how hot your oven is), or until the base is crisp and the topping cooked. Drizzle with oil.

SAUSAGE AND TOMATO PIZZA

MAKES 1 X 30 CM (12 INCH) PIZZA

200 g (7 oz) tinned chopped tomatoes
2 Italian sausages
1 x 30 cm (12 inch) pizza base (see page 125)
½ teaspoon dried oregano
8 black olives
extra virgin olive oil, for drizzling

1 **Preheat the oven** to very hot and put a baking tray or pizza stone in the oven to heat up.

2 **Mix the tomatoes** to a pulp in a food processor or push through a sieve. Remove the sausage skins and break the meat into pieces.

3 **Spread the tomato pulp** over the pizza base. Scatter with the sausage pieces, oregano and olives, and season. Slide onto the hot tray or stone (if you're not confident doing this, you can construct and bake the pizza on a cold tray, but the base won't be as crisp).

4 **Cook** for 2–12 minutes (this will depend on how hot your oven is), or until the base is light brown and crisp and the topping is cooked. Before serving, drizzle with a little extra virgin olive oil.

CANEDERLI

SERVES 4

4 garlic cloves

500 ml 17 fl oz/2 cups) milk

1 small sage sprig

10 g (¼ oz) dried porcini mushrooms

1 tablespoon olive oil

150 g (5½ oz) smoked pancetta or
  bacon, finely chopped

1 onion, finely chopped

2 carrots, finely chopped

2 celery stalks, finely chopped

1 tablespoon rosemary, finely chopped

400 g (14 oz) fresh breadcrumbs

50 g (1¾ oz) parmesan cheese, grated,
  plus extra to serve

½ teaspoon freshly grated nutmeg

1 egg

TO SERVE

1 litre (35 fl oz/4 cups) chicken stock

¼ small savoy cabbage, finely chopped

2 tablespoons chopped flat-leaf (Italian)
  parsley and grated parmesan cheese,
  to serve

1 Halve 2 garlic cloves and put them in a saucepan with the milk and the sage. Bring to a simmer, then remove from the heat and leave for 10 minutes to infuse. Cover the porcini with 3 tablespoons boiling water and leave to soak for 15 minutes.

2 Heat the oil in a saucepan, add the pancetta and onion and cook until the pancetta is light brown and the onion soft. Finely chop the remaining garlic and add to the pan with the carrot, celery and rosemary. Season and cook for about 15 minutes or until soft.

3 Drain the porcini, reserving the soaking liquid, and finely chop. Add to the vegetables, then pour in the soaking liquid, discarding any sediment at the bottom of the bowl. Simmer until all the liquid has evaporated. Set aside.

4 Put the breadcrumbs in a bowl and strain the infused milk over them. Mix well to soften and flavour the bread, then squeeze out the excess milk. Mix the vegetables with the bread, Parmesan, nutmeg and egg. Season, then refrigerate for 15 minutes. Shape into balls the size of table tennis balls.

5 Bring a large saucepan of salted water to a simmer. Add the dumplings in batches and cook until they float to the surface. Remove with a slotted spoon to drain.

6 Bring the stock to the boil and add the cabbage. Cook for 5–10 minutes or until tender. Add the dumplings and serve with a little extra parmesan and chopped parsley.

Note: Canederli are large, round bread dumplings. They can be served in a broth, as in this recipe.

SERVES 4

cornmeal

½ quantity pizza dough (see page 125)

1½ tablespoons olive oil

MOZZARELLA AND PROSCIUTTO CALZONE

170 g (6 oz) mozzarella, cut into 2 cm (¾ inch) cubes

2 thin slices prosciutto, cut in half

1 artichoke heart, marinated in oil, drained and cut into 3 slices from top to bottom

POTATO, ONION AND SALAMI CALZONE

2 tablespoons vegetable oil

1 small onion, very thinly sliced

75 g (2½ oz) small red potatoes, unpeeled, very thinly sliced

75 g (2½ oz) mozzarella cheese, cut into 2 cm (¾ inch) cubes

60 g (2¼ oz) sliced salami

2 tablespoons grated parmesan cheese

1 **Preheat the oven** to 230°C (450°F/Gas 8). Lightly oil a baking tray and dust with cornmeal. On a lightly floured surface, roll out the dough to form an 18 cm (7 inch) circle. Using the heels of your hands and working from the centre outwards, press the circle out to a diameter of about 30 cm (12 inches). Transfer to the baking tray. Lightly brush the entire surface with the oil.

2 **To make the mozzarella and prosciutto calzone,** spread the mozzarella cheese over half the dough circle, leaving a narrow border around the edge. Roll the prosciutto into little tubes and arrange on top of the cheese. Top with the artichoke slices and season well.

3 **Fold the other side** of the circle over the filling to make a half-moon shape. Match the cut edges and press them firmly together. Fold them over and press into a scrolled pattern to thoroughly seal in the filling. Brush the surface with a little extra olive oil, then transfer to the oven. Bake for about 20 minutes, or until the crust is golden.

4 **To make the potato, onion and salami calzone,** heat the oil in a frying pan and add the onion. Cook for 1 minute, then scatter the potato on top. Cook, stirring, for 3–4 minutes, until beginning to brown. Season, then spread over half the dough circle, leaving a narrow border around the edge. Scatter with the mozzarella, followed by the salami slices and Parmesan.

5 **Fold the other side** of the circle over the filling to make a half-moon shape. Match the cut edges and press them firmly together. Fold them over and press into a scrolled pattern to thoroughly seal in the filling. Brush the surface with a little extra olive oil, then transfer to the oven. Bake for about 20 minutes, or until the crust is golden.

PANINI WITH PROSCIUTTO AND ARTICHOKE

SERVES 4

2 bread rolls (see page 124)

2 teaspoons olive oil

4 slices prosciutto

2 artichoke hearts in olive oil

1 **Slice each roll in half,** leaving it joined along one long side like a hinge (this will help keep the roll together when you eat it).

2 **Drizzle a little olive oil over each cut surface.** Fold 2 slices of prosciutto onto each roll. Slice the artichoke hearts and divide them between the rolls. Season well. Fold the tops back on the rolls and press down firmly.

3 **Serve the panini straight away**—if they are left to sit they can become soggy.

Note: Panini should not be overstuffed or the filling will fall out when you try to eat them. They are great for lunches or picnics—if you're making a large number, arrange them in a basket or on a platter, half-wrapped in white paper napkins with the tops twisted.

PANINI WITH SALAMI AND PROVOLONE

SERVES 4

2 bread rolls (see page 124)

2 teaspoons olive oil

6 slices salami

4 thin slices provolone or mature
   pecorino cheese

1 **Slice each roll** in half, leaving it joined along one long side like a hinge (this will help keep the roll together when you eat it).

2 **Drizzle a little olive oil** over each cut surface. Layer the salami and cheese in the rolls and season well. Fold the tops back on the rolls and press down firmly.

Note: These panini can be prepared a few hours in advance without becoming soggy. Often the fillings for panini are very simple and this one is a classic example—slices of salami and cheese. There are lots of different types of salami to choose from, you just have to decide whether you're in the mood for a spicy type or something milder.

PANINI WITH CAPSICUM, ROCKET AND OLIVES

SERVES 4

2 bread rolls (see page 124)

2 teaspoons olive oil

½ yellow and ½ red capsicum (pepper),
   grilled and skinned

handful of rocket (arugula) leaves

6 black olives, pitted and cut into slices

1   Slice each roll in half, leaving it joined along one long side like a hinge (this will help keep the roll together when you eat it).

2   Drizzle a little olive oil over each cut surface. Slice the peppers, then divide them between the rolls. Add the rocket leaves, tearing them if they're large, and sprinkle with the olives. Season well. Fold the tops back on the rolls and press down firmly.

3   Serve the panini straight away—if they are left to sit they can become soggy.

Note: Rocket in Italy has a strong peppery flavour, which makes it the perfect partner for the sweetness of the grilled peppers. If you find the flavour of rocket too strong, you can use any other salad leaf that you prefer.

PANINI WITH GRILLED EGGPLANT AND MOZZARELLA

SERVES 4

2 bread rolls (see page 124)

2 teaspoons olive oil

6 slices grilled eggplant (aubergine)

6 slices mozzarella cheese

1 **Slice each roll in half,** leaving it joined along one long side like a hinge (this will help keep the roll together when you eat it).

2 **Drizzle a little olive oil over** each cut surface. Put 3 slices of grilled eggplant and 3 slices of mozzarella in each and season well. Fold the tops back on the rolls and press down firmly.

3 **Serve the panini** straight away—if they are left to sit they can become soggy.

Note: Bread rolls filled with all kinds of salumi (cooked meats), cheese and vegetables are a useful snack or quick lunch. In Italy, long white rolls are most often used. You can make your own, or buy them fresh. Grill the eggplant yourself, or buy them ready-prepared.

DESSERTS

TIRAMISU

SERVES 4

5 eggs, separated

180 g (6½ oz) caster (superfine) sugar

250 g (9 oz) mascarpone

250 ml (9 fl oz/1 cup) cold very strong coffee

3 tablespoons brandy or sweet Marsala

44 small sponge fingers

80 g (2¾ oz) dark chocolate, finely grated

1 **Beat the egg yolks** with the sugar until the sugar has dissolved and the mixture is light and fluffy and leaves a ribbon trail when dropped from the whisk. Add the mascarpone and beat until the mixture is smooth.

2 **Whisk the egg whites** in a clean dry glass bowl until soft peaks form. Fold into the mascarpone mixture.

3 **Pour the coffee** into a shallow dish and add the brandy. Dip some of the sponge finger biscuits into the coffee mixture, using enough biscuits to cover the base of a 25 cm (10 inch) square dish. The biscuits should be fairly well soaked on both sides but not so much so that they break up. Arrange the biscuits in one tightly packed layer in the base of the dish.

4 **Spread half the mascarpone** mixture over the layer of biscuits. Add another layer of soaked biscuits and then another layer of mascarpone, smoothing the top layer neatly. Leave to rest in the fridge for at least 2 hours or overnight. Dust with the grated chocolate to serve.

ZUPPA INGLESE

SERVES 4

CUSTARD

6 large egg yolks

100 g (3½ oz) caster (superfine) sugar

2 tablespoons cornflour (cornstarch)

1 tablespoon plain (all-purpose) flour

600 ml (21 fl oz) milk

½ vanilla pod or 1 teaspoon vanilla extract

1 ready-made 25 cm (10 inch) sponge cake (see page 157)

150 ml (5 fl oz) clear alcohol, such as grappa or kirsch

200 g (7 oz) raspberries

350 g (12 oz) blackberries

2 teaspoons caster (superfine) sugar

500 g (1 lb 2 oz) lightly whipped fresh cream, to serve

1 To make the custard, whisk the egg yolks with the sugar until pale and fluffy. Add the cornflour and flour and mix well. Heat the milk with the vanilla pod and bring just to the boil. Pour into the egg mixture, whisking as you do so. Pour back into the saucepan and gently bring to the boil, stirring all the time. Once the mixture is just boiling, take it off the heat and stir for another few minutes. Pour into a bowl and cover the surface with clingfilm to prevent a skin forming.

2 Slice the sponge into 2 cm (¾ inch) strips. Place a couple of pieces on each plate (you need to use deep plates) and brush with about 100 ml (3½ fl oz) of the alcohol. Leave to soak for at least 10 minutes.

3 Put the raspberries and blackberries in a saucepan with the remaining alcohol and the caster sugar. Gently warm through so that the sugar just melts, then set aside to cool. Spoon over the sponge, then pour the custard over the top of the fruit and serve immediately with the cream.

BAKED APPLES

6 cooking apples

75 g (2½ oz) unsalted butter, chilled

6 small cinnamon sticks

100 g (3½ oz) pistachio nuts or pine nuts

3 tablespoons brown sugar

100 g (3½ oz) raisins or sultanas

200 ml (7 fl oz) grappa

1 **Preheat the oven** to 175°C (350°F/Gas 4). Remove the cores from the apples with a sharp knife or corer and put them in an ovenproof dish.

2 **Divide the butter** into six sticks and push it into the cores of the apples. Push a cinnamon stick into the middle of each apple and scatter with the nuts, sugar and raisins. Finally, pour over the grappa.

3 **Bake** for 30–35 minutes, basting the apples occasionally with the juices in the dish until they are soft when tested with a skewer.

BAKED FIGS

SERVES 4

16 figs, halved

50 g (1¾ oz) hazelnuts

150 ml (5 fl oz) sweet Marsala

2 tablespoons honey

grated zest of 1 lemon and juice of
    ½ lemon

200 g (7 oz) mascarpone

1   **Preheat the oven** to 190°C (375°F/Gas 5). Arrange the fig halves in a buttered gratin dish large enough to fit them all snugly.

2   **Toast the hazelnuts** in the oven for 8 minutes, then chop them finely. Drizzle the Marsala and honey over the figs. Mix the lemon zest, hazelnuts and mascarpone together and spoon a little onto each fig. Sprinkle with the lemon juice.

3   **Bake** for about 25-35 minutes, or until the juices have reduced into a syrup and the figs are soft. Serve the figs with the juices poured over.

FRUIT POACHED IN RED WINE

SERVES 4

3 pears, peeled, quartered and cored

3 apples, peeled, quartered and cored

50 g (1¾ oz) sugar

1 vanilla pod, cut in half lengthways

2 small cinnamon sticks

400 ml (14 fl oz) red wine

200 ml (7 fl oz) dessert wine or port

700 g (1 lb 9 oz) red-skinned plums,
  halved

1 **Put the pears** and apples in a large saucepan. Add the sugar, vanilla pod, cinnamon sticks, red wine and dessert wine and bring to the boil. Reduce the heat and gently simmer for about 5-10 minutes, or until just soft.

2 **Add the plums,** stirring them through the pears and apples, and bring the liquid back to a simmer. Cook for another 5 minutes or until the plums are soft.

3 **Remove the saucepan** from the heat, cover with a lid and leave the fruit to marinate in the syrup for at least 6 hours. Reheat gently to serve warm or serve at room temperature with cream or ice cream and a biscuit.

SERVES 4

| 1 ready-made 25 cm (10 inch) sponge cake (see page 157) |
| 4 tablespoons sweet Marsala |
| 350 g (12 oz) ricotta cheese |
| 75 g (2½ oz) caster (superfine) sugar |
| ½ teaspoon vanilla extract |
| 100 g (3½ oz) mixed candied fruit (orange, lemon, cherries, pineapple, apricot), finely chopped |
| 50 g (1¾ oz) dark chocolate, chopped |
| green food colouring |
| 250 g (9 oz) marzipan |
| 2 tablespoons apricot or strawberry jam |
| 100 g (3½ oz) icing (confectioners') sugar |

1 **Use plastic wrap** to line a 20 cm (8 inch) round cake tin with sloping sides (a moule à manqué would be perfect). Cut the cake into 5 mm (¼ inch) slices to line the tin, reserving enough pieces to cover the top at the end. Fit the slices of cake carefully into the tin, making sure there are no gaps. Brush the Marsala over the cake in the tin, covering it as evenly as possible and reserving a little for the top.

2 **Put the ricotta** in a bowl and beat until smooth. Add the sugar and vanilla extract and mix well. Mix in the candied fruit and chocolate. Spoon the mixture into the mould, smooth the surface and then cover with the remaining slices of cake. Cover with plastic wrap and press the top down hard. Refrigerate for at least 2 hours, then unmould onto a plate.

3 **Knead enough green food colouring** into the marzipan to tint it light green. Roll out the marzipan in a circle until it is large enough to completely cover the top and side of the cassata. Melt the jam in a saucepan with 1 tablespoon of water and brush over the cassata. Position the marzipan over the top and trim it to fit around the edge.

4 **Mix the icing sugar** with a little hot water to make a smooth icing that will spread easily. Either pipe the icing onto the cassata in a decorative pattern, or drizzle it over the top in a crosshatch pattern. Serve immediately.

APRICOT AND ALMOND TART

SERVES 4

1 quantity sweet pastry (see page 157)

200 g (7 oz) dried apricots

100 ml (3½ fl oz) brandy or grappa

icing (confectioners') sugar, to dust

ALMOND FILLING

180 g (6 oz) softened unsalted butter

180 g (6 oz) caster (superfine) sugar

180 g (6 oz) flaked blanched almonds

2 eggs

1 teaspoon vanilla extract

1 heaped teaspoon plain (all-purpose)
   flour

1 **Grease** a 25 cm (10 inch) loose-bottomed metal tart tin. Lightly dust the work surface with flour and roll out the pastry until large enough to fit the tin. Line the tin and trim the edges with a sharp knife. If there is any leftover pastry, roll it thinly and cut into strips to lattice the top of the tart.

2 **Rest the pastry** in the fridge for 15 minutes or, if time is short, in the freezer until the pastry is firm. Preheat the oven to 200°C (400°F/Gas 6).

3 **Line the pastry shell** with crumpled greaseproof paper and baking beads. Blind bake the pastry for 12 minutes, then remove the greaseproof paper and, if the pastry still looks wet, dry it out in the oven for 5 minutes. Leave to cool for a few minutes. Reduce the oven to 180°C (350°F/Gas 4).

4 **While the pastry is cooling,** put the dried apricots and brandy in a saucepan and cook over low heat for about 5 minutes, or until most of the liquid has evaporated and just coats the apricots. Leave to cool.

5 **To make the almond filling,** use a food processor to cream the butter and sugar until light and pale. Add the almonds, eggs, vanilla and flour and briefly blend until just combined. If you overbeat it, the mixture may separate.

6 **Spoon the filling into the pastry shell,** then position the apricots in the tart shell, arranging them in two circles, one inside the other. Bake for 30-40 minutes, or until the filling is set and the top golden brown. If the top starts to get too brown cover it loosely with foil.

7 **Leave the tart to cool and sprinkle** with icing sugar just before serving. Serve with crème fraîche or cream.

FIG AND RASPBERRY CAKE

SERVES 4

185 g (6½ oz) unsalted butter
185 g (6½ oz) caster (superfine) sugar
1 egg
1 egg yolk
335 g (11¾ oz) plain (all-purpose) flour
1 teaspoon baking powder
4 figs, quartered
grated zest of 1 orange
200 g (7 oz) raspberries
2 tablespoons sugar

1   Preheat the oven to 180°C (350°F/Gas 4). Cream the butter and sugar in a bowl until light and pale. Add the eggs and beat again. Sift the flour over the bowl and fold in with the baking powder and a pinch of salt. Chill for 15 minutes until firm enough to roll out.

2   Lightly grease a 23 cm (9 inch) spring-form cake tin. Divide the dough in two and roll out one piece large enough to fit the base of the tin. Cover with the figs, orange zest and raspberries. Roll out the remaining dough and fit it over the filling. Lightly brush the dough with water and sprinkle with sugar.

3   Bake for 30 minutes, or until the top and bottom of the cake is cooked. Poke a skewer into the cake to see if it is ready—there should be no wet cake mixture clinging to the skewer. Serve with cream or mascarpone.

PANFORTE

SERVES 4

4 small sheets rice paper

100 g (3½ oz) skinned hazelnuts

100 g (3½ oz) blanched almonds

1 teaspoon each whole coriander seeds, cloves, nutmeg and black peppercorns

1 teaspoon ground cinnamon

50 g (1¾ oz) finely chopped dried figs

1 tablespoon cocoa

200 g (7 oz) roughly chopped candied orange and lemon peel

grated zest of 1 lemon

50 g (1¾ oz) plain (all-purpose) flour

150 g (5½ oz) sugar

4 tablespoons clear honey

2 tablespoons unsalted butter

icing (confectioners') sugar, to dust

1   **Butter and line the base** of a 20 cm (8 inch) spring-form cake tin with rice paper. Cut a few thin strips to line the side as well. Preheat the oven to 150°C (300°F/ Gas 3) and lightly brown the hazelnuts and almonds on a baking tray for about 6–8 minutes. Check often as the nuts can burn very quickly. Allow to cool.

2   **Grind the whole spices** together in a spice grinder or mortar and pestle. Put the nuts in a metal or china bowl with the spices, figs, cocoa, candied peel, lemon zest and flour and mix together.

3   **Put the sugar,** honey and butter in a heavy-based saucepan to melt, briefly stirring the butter into the sugar as it just starts to melt. Do not stir again or the sugar will crystallise. Bring to the boil and cook until the syrup reaches 120°C (245°F) on a sugar thermometer, or a little of it dropped into cold water forms a soft ball when moulded between your finger and thumb.

4   **Immediately pour the syrup** into the nut mixture and mix well, working quickly as it will soon cool and stiffen. Pour into the tin and smooth the top with a spatula.

5   **Bake** for about 15 minutes. Unlike other cakes, this will not colour or seem very firm, even when cooked, but will begin to harden as it cools. Allow to cool a little in the tin until it is firm enough to enable the side of the tin to be removed. If the mixture is still quite soft when cooled, place in the fridge to set. To serve, dust the top heavily with icing sugar.

PANNA COTTA

SERVES 4

450 ml (16 fl oz) thick (double/heavy)
   cream

4 tablespoons caster (superfine) sugar

2 tablespoons grappa (optional)

vanilla extract

3 leaves or 1¼ teaspoons gelatine

250 g (9 oz) berries, to serve

1   **Put the cream** and sugar in a saucepan and stir over gentle heat until the sugar has dissolved. Bring to the boil, then simmer for 3 minutes, adding the grappa and a few drops of vanilla extract to taste.

2   **If you are using the gelatine leaves,** soak them in cold water until floppy, then squeeze out any excess water. Stir the leaves into the hot cream until they are completely dissolved. If you are using powdered gelatine, sprinkle it onto the hot cream in an even layer and leave it to sponge for a minute, then stir it into the cream until dissolved.

3   **Pour the mixture** into four 125 ml (4 fl oz/½ cup) metal or ceramic ramekins, cover each with a piece of plastic wrap and refrigerate until set.

4   **Unmould the panna cotta** by placing the ramekins very briefly in a bowl of hot water and then tipping them gently onto plates. Metal ramekins will take a shorter time than ceramic to unmould as they heat up quickly. Serve with the fresh berries.

ITALIAN ORANGE BISCUITS

SERVES 4

175 g (6 oz) plain (all-purpose) flour

200 g (7 oz) semolina or fine polenta

100 g (3½ oz) caster (superfine) sugar

100 g (3½ oz) unsalted butter, softened

2½ teaspoons grated orange zest

2 eggs

1 **Put the flour,** semolina, sugar, butter, orange zest, eggs and a pinch of salt in a food processor and mix until smooth. Chill in the fridge for 15 minutes.

2 **Preheat the oven** to 190°C (375°F/Gas 5). Grease a baking tray and place a teaspoon of the mixture on the tray. Lightly moisten your fingers with a little water and press the mixture down to flatten it. Don't use too much water or it will affect the texture of the biscuits. Leave space between the biscuits as the biscuits will expand during cooking.

3 **Bake for about 15 minutes,** or until the edge of the biscuit is dark golden brown. Remove from the oven, scoop off the tray with a metal spatula and cool on a wire rack. If you are baking the biscuits in batches, make sure the tray is greased each time you use it. When cooled, store in an airtight container.

RICOTTA CAKE WITH ALMONDS AND CANDIED PEEL

SERVES 4

150 g (5½ oz) flaked or whole almonds

50 g (1¾ oz) pandoro sweet cake

6 eggs

100 g (3½ oz) caster (superfine) sugar

grated zest of 1 orange

grated zest of 1 lemon

500 g (1 lb 2 oz) ricotta cheese

200 g (7 oz) candied peel, chopped

icing (confectioners') sugar, to dust

1 **Preheat the oven** to 180°C (350°F/Gas 4). Toast the almonds on a baking tray in the oven for 8–10 minutes until golden brown. put the almonds and pandoro in a food processor and process until the mixture resembles coarse breadcrumbs. Alternatively, finely chop the nuts and pandoro and mix them together. Grease a 20 cm (8 inch) spring-form cake tin with a little butter. Tip some of the mixture into the tin and shake it around so that it forms a coating on the bottom and side of the tin. Put the remaining nut mixture aside.

2 **Whisk the eggs** and sugar for several minutes until pale and a little frothy. Add the orange and lemon zest, ricotta, candied peel and the remaining nut mixture and mix together very briefly.

3 **Pour into the tin and bake** for 40–50 minutes, or until the cake feels just firm to the touch. Cool in the tin. Dust with icing sugar before serving at room temperature.

BLOOD ORANGE GRANITA

SERVES 4

100 g (3½ oz) caster (superfine) sugar

400 ml (14 fl oz) blood orange juice
(about 5 oranges)

2 tablespoons Grand Marnier, vodka or
rum

grated zest of 2 oranges

1 **Heat the caster sugar** with 100 ml (3½ fl oz) of the orange juice in a saucepan until the sugar dissolves. Add the rest of the orange juice, the Grand Marnier and the orange zest and stir well.

2 **Pour into a plastic or metal freezer box.** The juice should be no deeper than 3 cm (1¼ inches) so that the granita freezes quickly and breaks up easily. Freeze overnight.

3 **Remove the granita** from the freezer and rake over it with a fork to break up the ice crystals. Return to the freezer and allow to chill for at least another 2 hours to solidify.

4 **Serve by raking the crystals again** and then spooning into chilled bowls. Granita melts very quickly so a chilled bowl will help it keep its shape a little longer.   •

CINNAMON GELATO

SERVES 4

1 vanilla pod
550 ml (19 fl oz) thick (double/heavy) cream
550 ml (19 fl oz) milk
2 cinnamon sticks
6 egg yolks
100 g (3½ oz) caster (superfine) sugar

1 **Split the vanilla pod down the middle,** leaving it joined at one end, and put in a saucepan with the cream, milk and cinnamon sticks. Bring just to the boil, then remove from the heat and leave to infuse for 1 hour.

2 **Whisk the egg yolks** and caster sugar in a large bowl until pale and creamy. Pour the milk over the egg yolk mixture and whisk quickly to combine.

3 **Pour the custard back** into the saucepan and cook over very low heat to just thicken it, stirring continuously with a wooden spoon. Remove from the heat and dip the spoon into the custard. Draw a line on the back of the spoon—if the line stays and the custard does not run through it, then it is ready, if not cook a little longer. Do not boil the custard or the eggs will scramble.

4 **Scrape the vanilla seeds** from the pod and mix them into the custard. Strain into a bowl, removing the vanilla pod and cinnamon sticks, and leave to cool. Churn in an ice-cream machine following the manufacturer's instructions. Alternatively, pour into a metal or plastic freezer box and freeze, whisking every 30 minutes to break up the ice crystals and give a creamy texture. Once set, keep in the freezer until ready to serve.

ZABAGLIONE

SERVES 4

6 egg yolks

3 tablespoons caster (superfine) sugar

125 ml (4 fl oz/½ cup) sweet Marsala

250 ml (9 fl oz/1 cup) thick (double/
heavy) cream

1 **Whisk the egg yolks** and sugar in the top of a double boiler or in a heatproof bowl set over a saucepan of simmering water. Make sure that the water does not touch the base of the bowl or the egg may overcook and stick. It is important that you whisk constantly to move the cooked mixture from the outside of the bowl to the centre.

2 **When the mixture is tepid,** add the Marsala and whisk for another 5 minutes, or until it has thickened enough to holds its shape when drizzled off the whisk into the bowl.

3 **Whip the cream until soft peaks form.** Gently fold in the egg yolk and Marsala mixture. Divide among four glasses or bowls. Cover and refrigerate for 3–4 hours before serving.

COFFEE GRANITA

SERVES 4

200 g (7 oz) caster (superfine) sugar

1.25 litres (44 fl oz/5 cups) very strong
  espresso coffee

1 **Heat the caster sugar** with 25 ml (1 fl oz) hot water in a saucepan until the sugar dissolves. Simmer for 3 minutes to make a sugar syrup. Add the coffee and stir well.

2 Pour into a plastic or metal freezer box. The mixture should be no deeper than 3 cm (1¼ inches) so that the granita freezes quickly and breaks up easily. Stir every 2 hours with a fork to break up the ice crystals as they form. Repeat this two or three times. The granita is ready when almost set but still grainy. Stir a fork through it just before serving.

ITALIAN BASICS

Grilling and peeling capsicums (peppers)

Cut the capsicums in half, trim off the membrane and scrape out the seeds. Put the capsicum cut side down under a very hot grill. Alternatively, grill the capsicum whole (this gives an even softer result as they steam from the inside).

Grill the capsicum until the skin is completely black and blistered. You may need to move them around a bit to make sure all the skin gets cooked.

Remove the capsicum from the grill and stack them up on top of each other or put them in a plastic bag—this will help the steam loosen the charred skin. Peel off the skin. Scrape off any stubborn bits with a knife.

Peeling chestnuts

Cut a cross in the flat side of each chestnut through the outer layer of skin. Soak the nuts in hot water for about 20 minutes, then drain.

Boil the nuts for 30 minutes or bake them at 200°C (400°F/ Gas 6) for 10-15 minutes or until the skin starts to peel backwards from the points of the cross.

Peel the skin off the nuts while they are still warm (this makes them easier to peel). If the second, thinner skin is still attached, boil the nuts for a couple of minutes to loosen it, then drain and rub away the skin with a tea towel (dish towel).

Chargrilling vegetables

Slice the vegetables to an appropriate thickness. Vegetables like potatoes should be thin enough for the heat to cook the middle before the outside burns. Small vegetables like baby onions can be skewered to hold them on the grill.

Heat a chargrill pan or barbecue until it is very hot. Don't brush the griddle or vegetables with oil or it will smoke and burn. Lay the vegetables on the grill: they won't stick if it is hot. When they are browned on one side, turn them over.

For the attractive cross-hatched pattern, wait until the first set of lines is marked, then turn the vegetable slices through 90 degrees and leave them to mark again.

Preparing asparagus

Remove the woody end of the asparagus by holding the asparagus with both hands and bending gently—the tough end of the asparagus will snap away at its natural breaking point.

Cook the spears for 1–2 minutes in simmering water, either by lying them flat in a frying pan or standing them upright in an asparagus steamer.

The spears are tender enough when they bend gently as you pick them up by the centre. They should still be bright green and the tips should still be intact. They can now be refreshed by plunging into cold water to stop the cooking process.

Making fresh egg pasta

Put 350 g (12 oz) doppio zero (00) pasta flour and 150 g (5½ oz) fine semolina in a bowl. Make a well in the middle and add 10 egg yolks and 3 whole eggs.

Mix the eggs together briefly. Using a spoon, flick a little of the flour into the egg mixture.

Using your hands, start to blend in the eggs with the flour and semolina, eventually kneading to form a ball of hard dough. Knead for about 5–10 minutes, or until the dough is smooth and velvety to the touch.

The dough should not stick to your finger if pressed in the middle. If it does stick, add more flour and continue kneading.

Cover the dough with plastic wrap and rest for 1–4 hours, depending on when you want to use it. You can leave the dough overnight but no longer or it will start to oxidise and black spots will appear.

Rolling out fresh pasta dough

Divide the pasta into six to eight flattened rectangular pieces and cover with plastic wrap to prevent drying out.

Dust the work surface with semolina. Flatten the first segment of pasta so that it is easier to roll through the machine.

Feed the pasta through the rollers on the widest setting. Fold the flattened pasta in half or thirds, so that it fits across the rollers. Repeat this process three times to create a velvety texture.

Making risotto

Use a large deep frying pan or shallow saucepan with a heavy base. Make sure the stock or liquid you are going to add is hot — keep it at a low simmer on the stove.

Cook the rice in the butter first. This creates a seal around the grains, trapping the starch. Stir frequently, not only to prevent the rice from sticking to the bottom of the pan but to ensure all the grains are cooked evenly.

Add the liquid a ladleful at a time. Stir constantly so that the rice cooks evenly and releases some of the starch, giving the risotto a creamy consistency. If you cook the rice too slowly, it will become gluey; too fast and the liquid will evaporate — keep it at a fast simmer.

Season the rice early on while it is absorbing flavour. Once it is cooked and the grains saturated, it won't soak up the seasoning as well. Taste the liquid around the rice to check the seasoning after the first couple of ladles of stock.

Don't swamp the rice with too much liquid, but add just enough to cover it so it cooks evenly. Once you have used nearly all the stock, start tasting the rice to prevent overcooking. The rice should be al dente.

It is impossible to gauge the exact amount of stock you might require. Stop cooking the rice as soon as it is creamy but still has a little texture in the middle of the grain. The risotto should be rich and thick like porridge, not too wet or dry.

Shaping suppli and arancini

Roll a small amount (about 50 g/1¾ oz) of cooked, cooled risotto into a ball about the size of a walnut.

Press a hole in the middle of the ball with your thumb. Place a small amount of filling (often a cube of cheese) into the middle and press the risotto rice back around it to reform the ball.

Press the risotto rice firmly so it is compact. Roll each ball in flour, egg and breadcrumbs, pressing so the crumbs attach themselves to the rice.

Making polenta

Put the specified amount of cold water and salt in a deep heavy-based saucepan and bring to the boil. Add the polenta in a steady stream, using a wooden spoon to stir the water vigorously as you pour the polenta in.

As soon as you have added all the polenta, reduce the heat so the water is just simmering and keep stirring for the first 30 seconds to prevent lumps.

The finished texture of the polenta will improve the more you stir it. Leave it to bubble away for about 40 minutes, stirring every few minutes to prevent it sticking. When cooked, it should be thick enough to fall from the spoon in lumps.

Shaping polenta

Polenta can easily be moulded into shapes for layering with sauce. Pour the polenta into a deep serving dish. You want it to be no more than 2.5 cm (1 inch) thick.

The polenta will mould itself into the shape of the dish. Allow to cool completely. Once cooled, the polenta is wonderfully pliable and easy to handle.

To slice, carefully turn the polenta upside down out of the dish and onto a board. Use a long sharp knife to slice it. The polenta slices can then be layered with sauce and reformed in the dish.

Butterflying fish

Gut small fish such as sardines through the belly and remove the head by snapping and pulling it off.

Pull the stomach apart gently and place the fish down on its opened stomach. Press your finger down on either side of the backbone to help loosen it.

Turn the fish the other way up and gently pull the backbone out through the belly. You may need to pinch it off at the tail end. Leaving the tail attached to the fillets make them look more attractive.

Filleting small fish

Fillet the fish by running your thumbnail or a knife along each side of the backbone through the skin. Pull the head upwards. The head, bones and guts should all come away together.

Scaling and gutting fish

The best way to remove scales is with a fish scaler. Hold the fish's tail and, lifting it slightly, scape against the direction of the scales. Alternatively, run the back of a knife firmly over the skin against the direction of the scales to scrape them off.

Using a pair of scissors, snip from the vent along to the gills, along the soft belly and remove the guts. Snip the gills out by pulling back the flap that covers them.

Trim the end of the tail and trim off any side fins. Leave the dorsal fin (the fin at the top) as this is a useful gauge during cooking — it pulls out easily once the fish is cooked through.

Spatchcocking poultry

Split the bird by cutting down each side of the backbone with a sharp knife or pair of poultry shears. Discard the backbone.

Put the bird cut side down on your chopping board and press firmly down on the rib cage, squashing it out flat. Trim off the wing tips and any excess fat or skin.

Baking a sponge cake

Grease a 25 cm (10 inch) round cake tin or loaf tin with a little butter. Line the base of the tin with greaseproof paper. Grease the paper and then lightly dust with flour.

Cream together 150 g (5½ oz) butter and 175 g (6 oz) caster (superfine) sugar until pale and creamy by beating it with a wooden spoon or with an electric whisk.

Add 3 room-temperature eggs, one at a time, beating each one in thoroughly.

Sift 250 g (9 oz) plain (all-purpose) flour, a pinch of cinnamon and 1 teaspoon baking powder into the bowl and lightly fold. Add 50 ml (1¾ fl oz) milk, folding it in gently.

Spoon into the cake tin, filling it no more than three-quarters full or the cake may ooze over the sides of the tin as it cooks.

Bake for 30-40 minutes at 180°C (350°F/ Gas 4), or until a skewer inserted into the middle comes out clean. Turn out onto a wire rack to cool.

Making sweet pastry

Rub 100 g (3½ oz) unsalted butter into 200 g (7 oz) plain (all-purpose) flour with your fingertips until the texture resembles fine breadcrumbs.

Stir in 50 g (1¾ oz) caster (superfine) sugar, 1 egg and 1 egg yolk and mix with the blade of a knife to form a dough.

Tip the dough out onto a lightly floured work surface and bring together with your hands to form a ball. Wrap in plastic wrap and rest for a minimum of 30 minutes or overnight.

INDEX